Driving Sales

WHAT IT TAKES TO SELL 1000
CARS PER MONTH

Chris J. Martinez

J. Joseph Group, LLC

Driving Sales: What It Takes to Sell 1000 Cars Per Month/ Chris J. Martinez—1st edition

ISBN 978-0-9979314-0-2

Contents

Dedicated to my wife and kids for pushing me, loving me and making me the happiest man on earth.

Introduction

I wrote this book so that others can benefit from the long hours and massive amount of research we have dedicated to developing our winning team at Charles Maund Toyota in Austin, TX. If you are a newcomer to this field, I want to give you a sense of direction—the kind of direction we weren't able to benefit from when we began our journey.

If you follow the steps outlined in this book, the only direction in which you can go is forward. I want to clarify exactly who should follow the steps outlined in the book, however. Although I've written it in a way that makes it most appropriate for beginners, the content is undeniably for every auto salesperson. Whether you know next to nothing about auto sales or are a successful sales manager, this book is for you.

If you are a casual reader and picked up this book simply because you had nothing better to do, you will find that it presents a large number of lessons. If you are a manager or sales executive, you might think you don't need a book like this. After all, why read something that was written with beginners in mind when you're not a beginner, but instead a successful salesperson. You're here because you know your game, and I respect that. But, trust me, you will still benefit if you want to consistently sell 1000 cars per month.

It might be tempting for you to jump to the end or skip the principles you think you know well. But, if you're not already consistently selling 1000 cars per month, something is missing. There is a key business principle you don't know about, have overlooked or aren't applying properly. This book will help you reevaluate your sales strategies, see where your processes differ from mine and determine what efforts produce the best results. Reading this book will enable you to give your customer the "Ritz-Carlton experience" and prevent your staff from being "budget motel" salespeople.

The first thing you must realize when you set out on this journey is, it is the people who make the biggest difference. The companies that forget this are the ones that go backward. These companies tend to focus only on increasing bottom-line savings by cutting employee costs, somehow not believing that they need their team players.

My experience proves that these companies are consistently doomed to fail, and this is why focusing on building the team is critical and precisely how we became one of the top 15 car dealerships in the nation. Marcus Lemonis had it right when he presented his Three Ps: People, Process and Product. These are the fundamentals of the journey I'll discuss through this book, and understanding and honing them is what will take you to the next level.

Before we begin, let me introduce myself a bit further. I grew up in El Paso, Texas—and not in the best environment. My mentality was hope for the best and prepare for the worst. I often found myself in sink-or-swim situations, and I was a great swimmer.

Years passed, and I met my wife. She was my motivator, my pillar and my biggest support. She helped me grow as a man, as a professional, as a husband and as the father I am today.

When I joined the car business, there was no roadmap to success for me to follow. I started with only a vision and an opportunity. We were ultimately able to take a team of people that was selling 100 new and 50 used cars per month to one that was selling 1000 cars per month (new and used, combined). It was not easy, but the hard work paid off.

I have now been in the car business for over twelve years. I started on the sales floor and moved up to the position I'm in today where I help run a dealership that is in the top fifteen out of more than 1250 stores nationwide.

There have been many people throughout my career who helped me get to the level I'm at today. The person who has been able to take me to the next level—and guide me while allowing me to think for myself—is my mentor, James M. "Jim" DiMeo. Jim always reminds me of a quote from Robert Kiyosaki:

A coach isn't your friend. A coach is there to push you beyond what you thought was possible or what you wouldn't do on your own.

This quote perfectly summarizes Jim's best quality. He pushed me as a manager more than anyone else did. He had a vision and took a leap of faith with me, and that's the reason I was able to help him develop our team. Today, our store is number one in the city, number one in the district, number three in the region and number 14 in the country. Our people have been a true inspiration in the area of teamwork. Without them, we would not have become the superstore we are today, and the longer we are together, the stronger we become.

My Journey to Charles Maund Toyota

While I presently work at the Charles Maund Toyota Dealership in Austin, Texas, I started my car-business career at a big-box retailer for used cars more than thirteen years ago. That is where I began my arduous learning process, but the truth is that even getting to that dealership is an interesting story in and of itself.

Up until that point, I worked various jobs while living in El Paso, Texas. My financial situation was tight, and I believed I needed to leave the area in order to make more money. My uncle had offered me a job in his construction business in Las Vegas, Nevada, and while I wasn't excited about the venture, I needed to support my family.

When I arrived in Vegas, I wasn't particularly sold on the idea of working for the family business. It was almost through sheer luck that my twin brother asked me if I would consider working for a car dealership. I was reluctant at first, but the urge to avoid working in construction was greater than that reluctance, and I was up for a new challenge.

My brother mentioned that this particular dealership seemed different in concept from the horror stories we had heard about car sales. He had an appointment for an interview, but asked me to go in his place. I had a choice to make: start out in construction the next day or try out this new opportunity. I didn't think this new opportunity could hurt, and I believed that my uncle would understand. So I took the next step and accepted the job.

The management greeted me at the hotel where the meeting was to take place, and I told them that while I wasn't sure about this business, a guy named Terry was trying to recruit my twin brother, and I came in his place. They had a good chuckle about it and began to brief me about this career path. I distinctly remember a good friend of mine saying to me, "Chris, you look like a car salesman," and I was pretty upset that he had said that because of the stereotype that seems to follow car salespeople. I needed the money, however, and listening to them speak about the opportunity made me realize that I had the potential to make twice as much as I would in construction. So I agreed, not realizing that this tiny opportunity would later become my defining career path.

I worked with that dealership for the next six years, learning about every aspect of the business. I saw the company grow from 30 to 115 stores, and watching that growth prepared me for my future position. It was, in essence, my college education. They taught me well, and I was sad when I had to leave, but I believe that when one door closes, another opens.

As a manager for many years, I was given the opportunity to work with an up-and-coming Toyota Dealership on the sales floor, which was an adjustment. I had always heard that, in a traditional dealership environment, I could make a pretty good living. I quickly caught on while working on the sales floor, and I was selling a lot of cars. As a sales professional, I was able to double my income almost instantly, although it wasn't easy.

I received a lot of criticism from my coworkers. I had never before been disliked, so that criticism was extremely unsettling. I was called it all, from "Cheese Man" to "Mr. Spoon." It was hurtful, and I felt harassed in a way I never before had. People couldn't believe that someone who simply came in and put in the work was outselling them right away. These were some of the bitterest moments of my career, and I considered not including them in this book. But I want to reinforce the message that you should never give up. Keep pushing forward. Not everyone will like you. Stay focused on the task at hand, and good things will come.

My Internet Director introduced me to the principles that encouraged the dealership's Internet and walk-in customers to come in. The information was fascinating. I spent a lot of time with her and helped her in her efforts to push more traffic to the dealership. Doing this also helped me focus more on the best ways to sell cars and develop my own sales strategy. She saw my potential—combined with all of my dealership experience—and decided to have a conversation with my General Manager.

My Desk Manager had begun to take notice as well, and with help from both of them, I was able to sell more than 30 cars per month. We had our process down. A year and a half into this new job, my General Manager, Jim, decided to take a chance on me, and made me the manager at one of his used car lots.

The next six months were the hardest of my career, but I considered it a great education for what would come. After my time managing the used car lot, I asked to go back to selling cars. When I returned, it was as though I had never left. I stepped back onto the sales floor and sold 30 cars in the first month—and then every month thereafter. I was officially a member of the 30-Car Club. In my last month on the floor, I sold 35.5 cars, and Jim called me into his office and said, "Chris, I just became a buying partner for a Toyota Dealership in Austin, Texas, and I want you to come with me."

I confessed that I thought there were only two stores in Austin, and I had never heard of the one he was talking about. I asked him to give me the evening to think about it and discuss it with my wife, and he agreed. He said, "Keep in mind, Chris. I can't pay you what you are making right away, but in two to three years, it will pay dividends." He always had a way of selling me on his dream, and I trusted him. He also asked our Desk Manager to go with him. My Desk Manager vowed, "Chris we're going to make it happen." I spoke to my wife that evening. She told me she was with me, and she was sure we could make it happen together. After having these conversations and putting my faith in God, I resigned the next morning from San Antonio and moved to Austin. It was one of the scariest things I've done, but I knew if Jim had that much faith in my abilities and my wife was behind me, I would have faith as well.

The first week at Charles Maund Toyota was so fun that I immediately wanted more responsibility. Jim supported all of my ideas, gave me valuable guidance whenever needed, and encouraged me to push my limits. Customers were always at the dealership; the dealership simply didn't have a team focused on them.

Grant Cardone proclaims in his fantastic book, *The 10x Rule*, "You have to 10X your actions." I needed this mantra like I needed air to breathe, and I followed it to a tee. We focused on developing our team and watching the numbers grow. It felt like we were in a movie. We knew what to do and how to get the dealership to the next level. We focused on increasing our staff and building an internet department. Ultimately, I created a tool called theautominer.com with Jim, and his son, James DiMeo Jr., was one of the key people who helped us in this endeavor. Theautominer.com is a database-mining tool designed to help us target customers, among other tasks. Through Jim's tremendous knowledge and talent, he helped me bring the vision to fruition.

The moment I walked into the Austin dealership, it felt as though I had walked back in time. Their processes were old, and they weren't focusing enough on the business end. They acted like fat cats with no ball of yarn to entice them into action. They had no incentives. Their employees were good, but they needed to be pointed in the right direction. We doubled their numbers overnight—not because we were better, but because we had our running shoes on.

In our first meeting, Jim told us that his target goal was to sell over 500 cars per month. Everyone looked at him like he was crazy, but I saw his vision and knew what it was going to take to achieve it. I told my wife that she probably wasn't going to see me for a while! I worked a lot of open-to-close days during that first year; we needed to start from scratch and push our sales guys to make phone calls and follow our proven process.

Many of the employees jumped ship early on. They weren't used to coaches pushing them outside of their comfort zone, and as Cardone says, "Comfort zones are where dreams go to die." I believe that wholeheartedly, and I believe that something's wrong with me if I don't believe that my job is constantly in danger.

Our first challenge was to hire employees with the same drive we had. What we wanted was a winning team. If you want to start a successful team, do not pick players who can't run fast or don't know how to kick. We applied this concept in developing our team. The people we chose didn't have to be the best; they simply needed to have a hunger for results, a passion and a desire. This hunger, passion and desire were the reasons that, in our first year, we broke every record the store had. But it wasn't until a year and eight months later that we reached 500 cars per month. It was hard. But we focused on the Two Ps—the People and Process—to take us there.

Once we reached our goal of 500 cars per month, we set our sights higher. We reached 600 cars per month within the second year. Passing this mark was even harder because, in our third year, we not only had to think about moving forward but also about sustaining sales up to the 500- to 600-cars-per-month mark.

The milestone that followed required structural and functional changes. We had to figure out how to expand our workstations and further improve our processes. As a result, we broke the 800 cars-per-month mark. And, by our official 4-year anniversary, we had surpassed the 960 cars-per-month mark, which proved much more difficult than we initially thought because we didn't yet have the adequate processes in place to be a 900-car store. Therefore, it took us four more months to again cross the 900 mark. Three months later, we were finally able to break the 1020 cars-per-month mark. So, all tolled, it took us four years and seven months to be able to claim that we were a 1000 car-per-month store.

Looking back, it seems pretty remarkable (almost unbelievable, in fact) that, within merely four years, we took a store that was selling only 150 new and used cars in a single month to one that was consistently able to sell more than 1000 cars per month. It took not only the right leadership but also a shared team vision in order to reach that point.

Developing a Winning Team

Developing a team at a car dealership involves the same basic steps as does developing any other sales team in any other industry. Gathering a group of the right kind of professionals to do an efficient job can be haphazard and chaotic at first, and there's no definitively "right" way to go about it. You may be a manager, a director or a single salesperson who needs to develop a team from scratch. You may be hired specifically to build a new team or to re-organize an existing one. Either way, the process can feel like pandemonium. But, amidst all the commotion, what must guide you is your goal: selling 1000 cars per month. That is the finish line, the ultimate destination, the bull's-eye, the Holy Grail. The goal is everything. Whatever else you need to do must be a step forward in the pursuit of that goal.

It is essential, therefore, before taking any action while developing a team, to ask yourself this question: does this step bring me closer to my goal? If the answer is yes, then go right ahead! There may be tough decisions ahead. You may need to fire some people, and you may need to place restrictions on others. You may need to push everyone further and further still beyond what they believe they're capable of. They may appear to hate you for it. But remember, your goal is not love; your goal is results.

You cannot be afraid to buy inventory, and you need owners with brass balls. Salespeople might not like you, but your toddlers don't necessarily like you when you're forcing them to take medicine, either. Push your staff to take that medicine, and then let them love you when payday comes. Let that payday show them that it was all worth it. I've been broke, and I've heard the saying "money doesn't buy you happiness, but being broke doesn't either." It is necessary to push your team to keep them financially healthy.

When developing the team, remember that car sales is a performance-based business. You have to set goals for your people and, if they don't hit those goals, you have to upgrade and find better players. The NFL and all major-league sports teams maintain this philosophy, and I recommend working your business the same way. It's easier said than done, however. I have had to let go of people who I really liked but who simply couldn't quite "get it." The sales people have to understand that, if they don't make money, management will fire them. Also, make sure your pay-plan is set above the rest. That's a surefire way to attract and retain the best of the best.

THE FOUR STAGES OF TEAM DEVELOPMENT

In 1965, Bruce Tuckman proposed a model that listed four stages of team development: forming, storming, norming and performing. According to Tuckman, these stages are crucial and unavoidable in the process of team development. Any team needs to progress, face challenge, find solutions and achieve results. Let's see what happens when we implement Tuckman's model in the automotive sales industry:

FORMING

In the forming stage, the team meets, understands and agrees on the goals, learns about the potential challenge and begins the journey toward the achievement of the stated goals. In car sales, this process begins when you start hiring new salespeople for your teams. In the hiring process, you must be upfront. You must clearly present your goals as well as the challenges a new salesperson may face. This step is crucial; if team members are not aware of potential challenges when they come on board, they may blame you or the management for it later. This can create an unwanted and messy situation later and, in order to avoid that, you want to ensure that you hire only those who are fully aware of the risks and challenges and want to work with you to achieve your goals.

Even after you hire people who are talented and motivated, they may still be relatively uninformed about the actual objectives of the team or the right way to go about achieving them (or the issues they may face along the way). We generally refer to this time period as "the calm before the storm."

STORMING

This stage is the hardest. It is the stage during which conflicts arise that will force you to step up and assert yourself as a leader and lay down the rules of your game.

Let's assume you hired what you believe is a generally capable and "good" team, overall. The Storming stage is when you go from good to great. It's also filled with disagreements, disdain and discord. During this time, your salespeople will form opinions about one another's characters, abilities and responsibilities. Differences will arise, and questions will be raised. It will be up to you to solve all these problems and pave the way forward.

The length of the Storming stage depends upon team members' character as well as the nature of your leadership. Some teams don't come of this stage intact, and it may be necessary to start anew, while some teams start off already efficient enough that they jump straight over this stage and go straight into Norming.

NORMING

Once disagreements have been resolved and personality clashes have been mitigated, the team will begin to grow closer. It will begin to be aware of the competition and members will begin to tolerate one another. They may even grow to like one another! Your role in the Norming stage is to take all team members' differences into account and make new rules. Find the problems, and offer the solutions. Ensure the smooth functioning of the sales process so that it operates like a well-oiled machine.

PERFORMING

Once the storm is over and the dust has settled, your team will begin to perform. This is the business stage. This is where the action occurs, roles are established and responsibilities are distributed. This is also the time when individual members of your team will start to shine. Someone sold 20 cars in a month? You push them toward 30. Someone cannot get past the 10 cars-per-month mark? You identify the problems and guide them to the next 10.

Don't rush or push them too hard at this point, but don't relax and let them lag behind either. One step at a time, your process will be a constant, self-correcting mechanism.

5 STEPS TO CREATING A WINNING TEAM

The aforementioned stages showcase a general outline of how team development is managed. You may be feeling, however, that the described approach is great, but too abstract. You may be wondering, "What are some of the tangible steps I can take?" Don't worry. I have a list of key measures you should carry out while developing the perfect sales team.

BE SMART WHILE HIRING

A good hiring mechanism is the backbone of an efficient team development process. It is grueling and, in the automotive sales industry, it's even harder since there is no college degree offered in the area of car sales.

Therefore, what are some of the merits that a good salesperson must possess? Experience is the first that comes to mind. Prior sales experience can be a plus, but it's not everything, as some potentially good candidates may have no sales experience at all; they may not even have a sales background. On the other hand, some of the more experienced salespeople may think they have it all figured out. They may be too arrogant or overly confident. So you need to ask yourself, "Is this person coachable?"

ESTABLISH PERFORMANCE INDICATORS

Once you have hired a professional team, you cannot let them run wild or go rogue. You must rein them in through the establishment of a set of Key Performance Indicators (KPIs). These indicators do not necessarily have to be the numbers of cars sold in a month (although that is the most important one). Be creative in setting your KPIs.

They might be quantitative (number of car sales in a month) or qualitative (quality of salesmanship). It is vital that you make sure that the whole team understands and diligently follows the KPIs. Make monthly sales charts, daily summaries and weekly reports. You can even hire specialists to evaluate team performance. If you don't do all of that, well, there is no accountability!

Any sales activity (and any performance-based activity—not just car sales) is all about numbers. You have to know your numbers. You have to stick to those numbers. You have to evaluate your performance based on those numbers. But what exactly are these numbers?

Sales numbers are the goals you set for yourself regarding performance. For instance, in car sales, we operate based on the "4, 3, 2, 1" rule. In any given day, a salesperson must deal with 4 customers, go on 3 test drives, perform 2 write-ups and close 1 sale.

Those are the numbers. We know our numbers, and we stick to our numbers. This approach enables us not only to constantly measure and refine our performance but also sustain sales at a desirable level. If you know your numbers, you can always increase your actions to meet your daily targets. You can work toward selling to more people.

NEVER LOWER YOUR TARGET

When it comes to setting out to achieve your targets, the best approach is to increase your actions. The burden of increased responsibilities on your shoulders can act as an additional incentive to excel.

COMMUNICATION IS KEY

If there is one quality that will hold your team together like Super Glue, it is effective communication. Without it, the entire structure will crumble like a house of cards in a gust of wind. You need to constantly communicate—not just with your sales team but with your customers, too. Guide your team members, receive feedback, revise your strategy and incorporate criticisms; don't let any problems fester; weed out the troublemakers; engage with your team on a personal level; and know the strengths and weaknesses of each team member. Once you are doing all of these things, you can start thinking about how to proceed forward.

MAKE SURE YOU HAVE THE RIGHT TOOLS

Imagine the sales process like fixing a door. You need a very specific set of tools to do the job. Although you could manage to do it even without the tools, the result would not be quick or efficient. Similarly, in sales you need a specially designed apparatus in order to improve both productivity and success.

You might wonder what exactly these tools are, and you can rely on one or several tailor-made solutions ranging from a customer database to data mining programs.

I created a database-mining tool I mentioned earlier, theautominer.com, which helped me target our customers in unique ways in order to help increase retention. After all, it's one thing to sell your customer one car, and it's another thing to keep selling them cars. I have more than 140,000 people in our customer database, which not only enables us to target the right people but also perform automated database marketing. For instance, we can easily filter out customers who purchased a particular kind of product.

It is imperative to note at this point that this or any other software alone will not magically resolve all of your problems. Simply having an IT department won't boost sales. You must be involved in every step of the process. You must invest time and effort to come up with innovative ideas. Being involved with the software development team is, however, the key to obtaining a specific toolkit to better suit your unique needs.

THE SALES PROCEDURE

It's important to note that creating a winning sales team is not the be-all-end-all solution to the problem of needing to increase monthly sales; it is simply the tool that will allow you to successfully implement the solutions. Once you have a team established, you can take the next step forward—roll up your sleeves, move up a gear and accelerate to full capacity.

This likely sounds appealing, but how exactly do you achieve it? The answer is simple: focus on my four stages of the sales process, and push your sales team into performance mode. Breaking down your sales process into a particular number of steps is essential in order to better identify the problem areas and evaluate your approach to any one of these steps without having a spillover effect into other areas. The following is a list of the four stages of a sales process and details on how they will be further explained in the coming chapters.

THE PROCESS

The first step to boosting sales is having a definite and distinct sales process. A sales process is a defined set of steps your sales team follows from the time they are working on early-stage prospects all the way to the point when they turn them into a closed customer. Some of the common steps in a typical sales process include looking for potential prospects, connecting with early-stage leads to gather information, the actual formal demonstration of the vehicle you want to sell, closing the deal and following up with the customer.

You need to be mindful of some important considerations while formulating a sales process. The first of these considerations is the kind of business you have. This is what determines the nature of your sales process and which steps will receive maximum priority. For instance, in car sales a lot depends on the sociability and affability of the salesperson; it all comes down to presentation skills. Therefore, you would naturally pay more attention to the demonstration than, say, searching for newer prospects. Another consideration is the demands of changing circumstances; you must constantly review and revise your sales process in accordance with the new industry requirements

SALESMANSHIP

Salesmanship, as you know, involves the ability to convince or persuade people to buy a particular product. Increasing skills in this area is the most obvious step involved in boosting monthly sales and the most crucial one when it comes to the automobile industry. The first step in ensuring effective salesmanship is hiring a team of skillful salespeople. Once you have a team, all members must be on the same page regarding sales strategies, targets, dos and don'ts.

Successful salesmanship relies on a set of skills and techniques and, more importantly, understanding the proper time to utilize a specific skill or technique. Some of the skills required to be a prosperous salesperson include developing an understanding of the customer's demands; being trustworthy; having demonstrative skills; being helpful, friendly, and sociable; taking the prospects to the next stage; and being professional.

The traditional view of salesmanship in the car business is: customer walks in, salesman makes the pitch, salesman closes the deal, customer walks out with the product and salesman counts the money. That may have been accurate 10 years ago, but times have changed. These days, salesmanship is involved in every stage of the sales process, including the stage before any contact with a prospective buyer. Finding prospects, formal demonstrations, closing the deal and then following up all depend on good salesmanship.

A true sales professional understands the psychology of the customer. This enables him to better understand how to close the deal. RC Evans first told me about a mechanism that identified four different types of customers. The D.E.C.S system helps you truly understand how to mirror your customers.

D - Dominant/Driver. When you work with this sort of customer, you have to act like them.

E - Ego/Expressive. If you want to close the sale with this person, you need to stroke their ego.

C - Complacent/Amiable. You need to approach these people in more general, human terms—not through a business approach.

S - Stable/Analytic. This customer needs to know the numbers, and you need to demonstrate every scenario to them. If you want to close more sales, you need to know and understand these four types of customers.

The VAK tool is also helpful. You must understand the following three learning styles:

Visual learning: For people to better understand what you are saying, you have to write down things as you talk.

Auditory learning: You have to speak up to get your message across.

Kinesthetic learning: This is a combination of both visual and auditory learning whereby customers understand you better when you speak while interacting with physical objects for both audio and visual signals.

CLOSING THE SALE

You made a terrific presentation, and the customer is willing to buy. You are happy. Your job is over, right? Wrong. Closing the sale is one of the most critical steps of the entire process. It's make or break, do or die. Sealing the deal is, in and of itself, an art. Here, too, we need a combination of skills and techniques.

In a later chapter, I will present a list of top closing techniques that have worked for my team and me to boost sales from 150 to 1000 cars per month (and sustaining monthly sales at that level). The list includes:

Opinion close: you ask the customer's opinion regarding the hurdles to closing the deal

Assumptive close: you are confident that the customer will make the decision to buy the product

Now-or-Never close: you set a particular timeline such as "limited discount offers" to persuade the customer to sign the deal

Balance-sheet close: you make a list of pros and cons to persuade prospective buyers

I will describe five steps you need to take in order to close car deals, including pulling out the worksheet, filling in the equipment list, determining the starting price, filling in the customer details and writing personalized notes on the dealership worksheet. I'll also discuss five common mistakes to avoid while closing a deal. These include attempting to close too soon, trying to close with the wrong person, waiting for too long to close, failing to notice the close and continuing to sell after the close.

You need to know every customer so fluidly that if one raises an objection, you are on your counter in an instant to overcome it. It's like a boxing match. If someone connects a right hook, you've got to be able to counter it or you'll get knocked out. The *Closers Survival Guide* by Grant Cardone is a must-read on this subject. It is a truly informative and engaging read.

THE FOLLOW-UP

While it is not easy to sell 1000 cars in a month, it is even more difficult to sustain sales at that level. For that reason, your follow-up game must be strong. Before we proceed to surgically examine some of the best ways to enhance sales through follow-up, however, we need to ask ourselves "What exactly is follow-up, and why do we need good follow-up?" It is critical to determine the requirements of a good follow-up.

The first step in ensuring successful follow-up is identifying and classifying different types of leads. Having a comprehensive customer database is a pre-requisite for successful follow-up. It is important to accurately time the follow-up based on the customer's needs. It is also essential to ask whether integrating marketing and sales can produce the best results. Moreover, incorporating education, repetition and variety can produce the best results.

FOUR STAGES OF
A WINNING SALES PROCEDURE

STAGE 1: THE PROCESS

If you have a skilled team and the right tools, you are prepared to go to the next level. The next level is getting the team to perform at an optimal level. The first and most important requirement to positioning your team in a way that produces results is having a definitive sales process. A definitive sales process is not something that you come up with on the first day of work. A sales process emerges—somewhat organically—through rigorous experience, constant back and forth and relentless trial and error. This means that a process is never perfect, and it is in a state of constant evolution.

"Get back to the basics." That's one sentence you hear at almost every dealership—and for good reason. What is the relationship between the process and the basics of car sales? The process is the basics. Without it, you cannot even begin to imagine how to move forward. Without the process, the road map to the sale is unclear. Before we proceed further to the nitty-gritty of it, however, let us first define exactly what a sales process is.

WHAT DO I MEAN BY THE PROCESS?

The best way to attempt to define any term is to break it down and analyze every word's meaning or significance. In this case, we have two words: sales and process. Let's consider *sales* first. The term sales is rather obvious. It means that you have a product that you need to sell. In our case, those products are cars, and you need to sell 1000 of them in a month.

Process, however, is a bit trickier. Process requires that there must be a list of definite and, more importantly, repeatable steps. Those steps may be in a particular order, and one step may naturally lead to another.

But where does the process itself take us? The answer to that depends on the process's scope. Is it a macro process designed to lead us to improved sales, or is it a micro process designed to focus on the way each and every individual customer is managed? Although these approaches are contrasting, they are not mutually exclusive. You may follow a combination of both. Most sales individuals say that the results are the most important aspect. But I stress the latter approach because when you begin to focus on every single customer you currently have and every customer you can bring into the fold, it automatically leads to increased sales.

Therefore, our analysis reveals that "sales process" is a list of a fixed number of steps that lead us to increased sales. It focuses on how to begin with an early-stage prospect and make them, in an organized manner, a closed customer. An easy way to remember it is to think that sales are our goal; process is the way to achieve that goal.

How do you know which process is the right process? Some would suggest that whatever earns you the most money is the right process. And I would agree with that, for the most part. However, I think that the right process is not only what makes you rich but also what feels right. And this can take years to perfect. You must gradually ease into it until it fits you like a pair of well-worn shoes, until you're as comfortable in it as you are in your own skin, and until every aspect of the sales process functions as a well-oiled machine.

Components of an Effective Sales Process

There is no one-size-fits-all model for a sales process; every one is different and unique. However, there's a common thread that may be found, and we need to find that thread. We need to find the stages or steps that are involved in every sales process and then focus on each one individually. These are some of the components of a sales process:

PROSPECT

There are two ways of looking at prospects—as a means and as an end. We perform prospecting to find potential prospects. Who are those potential prospects? Any person is a prospect if he or she meets three basic criteria:

- He must have the buying authority.
- He must have the financial capacity.
- He must have the willingness to purchase your products.

These three criteria make the difference between an uninterested individual and a potential customer.

How do you find prospects? There are a million good ways to seek prospects and no perfect way. You need to find what works best for you. You need a healthy combination of traditional means such as attracting the walk-in crowd through the sheer force of personality or non-traditional means like email or social media. Maintaining a functional customer database is crucial in finding prospects because your existing customers are your most valuable resources.

They are your brand ambassadors. They can be the ones who bring in the most referrals—depending on your service and reliability, of course.

CONNECT

Once you considerably narrow down your target audience to a manageable size, the next step is to connect with your prospects. When attempting to sell 1000 cars per month, a great deal of your success hinges on how well you connect with your leads. Your dealership or store may not be ideally placed to receive an abundance of walk-in traffic, and how can you sell 1000 cars in a month when you don't even have 1000 walk-in customers in a month?

The solution to this is to follow the ten-to-one rule. You must assume that, in an ideal situation, you'll close one deal for every ten leads with whom you connect. So if you need to sell 1000 thousand cars, and you have zero walk-in traffic, you must establish contact with 10,000 leads or prospects. It's a huge task, but I never promised it would be easy.

DEMONSTRATE

Ask anyone what image comes to his mind when he thinks about a car salesperson. Nine out of ten will describe a neatly dressed, professional-looking, friendly guy walking around a brand new car explaining its various features to an on-looking customer. The mere fact that this image is the first to spring to anyone's mind indicates how crucial the demonstration is. The practical vehicle demonstration is one of the most important aspects of car sales, but it is also the most neglected one. During my more than 12 years of experience, I have seen many dealerships that are ideally placed to receive a lot of walk-in traffic or work hard to secure or contact leads ultimately lose most customers during a demonstration or walk-around. It's surprising that they don't even realize what's going wrong!

Every salesperson needs to work on his demonstration skills. Without them, you simply cannot be successful. From the initial greeting or handshake to the price negotiation, every aspect of the demonstration is critical. It's a performance. Every move requires precision, and every problem or question demands skillful resolution.

For instance, consider the importance of knowing about the technical aspects of the vehicle. You must know everything, but you don't need to tell the customer everything. If you bombard the customer with every little technical detail, or try to use difficult jargon in order to sound impressive, you've already lost the customer. If you try to be too vague and skim over some of the crucial details, you've lost the customer. Or, let's say that you blurt out everything you know about the vehicle and then the customer asks a question. What do you do then? The knowledge you demonstrate must only be the tip of the iceberg. That way, if curious customers do ask a question, you can provide an in-depth answer that satisfies their concerns. As you can see, a successful demonstration requires balance, meticulousness and craft.

CLOSE

I have already touched upon the subject of closing a deal, and will discuss it in more detail later on. At this point, we need to consider how critical the role of closing the deal is in your overall process. I spoke about the process as a constant back and forth, a tweak here and a twist there. When, exactly, do you know that what your process lacks is a good close?

There are many different indicators that your close needs some tweaking. One such indicator is that a salesperson can easily bring the customers to the negotiating table, but cannot retain them beyond that. Another indicator is that a salesperson is too flexible in negotiating the price and is, therefore, letting most of the customers walk away with their preferred price.

How do you spot these problems? As a manager, you cannot sit in on every deal; it's not physically possible. This is the stage where the performance indicators we discussed earlier come into play. Some of those indicators can be designed to gauge the performance of the salesperson—not just on the floor but in the office as well.

FOLLOW UP

Sometimes what a good process needs most is a good follow-up. This is where you can transform a lead into a deal and one-time customers into long-time customers. A good follow-up is a critical component of the sales process since it lets you not only substantially increase the number of sales per month but also sustain that number of sales. You must be mindful of the fine line between maintaining and/or nurturing a relationship with a prospect and being bothersome or annoying.

How to Create a Sales Process

Now that you know what a sales process is and what some of its primary components are, how do you set out to create a process for your dealership? You may find yourself feeling clueless on that front, but do not freak out! The key is to just relax, take a breath and let the process come to you. How you take it forward depends upon your circumstances. You may be at the helm of a new business venture or taking over an unsuccessful or failing company. The latter is much more challenging than the former.

There are two ways to go about forming a process: transformation and optimization. These two distinct options may take you in entirely different directions. Transformation may include a major overhaul of the company's sales policies, procedures and practices. It is a change of approach that dictates a new agenda. In many ways, it is similar to beginning from scratch. Optimization, on the other hand, focuses only on the negatives while retaining the positives. Unlike transformation, it is a set of reforms rather than a revolution.

In either case, here are some of the things you can do to create a process of your own:

OBSERVE

If there's a single key to creating an efficient process, it's observation. Your observations are your data set, and they enable you to make better choices. Observe your past deals and highlight the negatives and positives. Observe the successes. Observe the flaws. Observe the activities of your team. Observe the feedback from the clients. The more you observe, the more room for improvement there becomes. Your observations must not be normative or prescriptive but merely statements of facts. They are if-then statements—if I do x, then y happens. For instance, if we do not offer discount to the clients, they buy from our competitor. The observations create clear, hard facts.

Another requirement is that your observations be accurate. If the discount is not the reason the customers prefer your competitor and the real reason is, say, bad service, then you'll never really be able to solve the problem. Making observations is crucial but making the right observations is even more important.

Another way to make observations is to ask a list of questions. How many cars did we sell each day? Which were some of the busiest days and why? Which were some of the slower days and why? How many customers walked in last month? How many of them bought vehicles? Why did a lot of them not buy? How did the customers feel about our prices and services? Which team member sold the most number of cars? Who sold the least? These are, of course, some of the standard questions that may provide a general overview of the business. And as the business progresses, the questions will begin to become much more specific and complex.

Once you have a set of reliable observations, you should proceed to the next step: Translate.

TRANSLATE

The second step of creating a sales process is much more difficult than the first. This step is point at which you translate your observations into practical solutions, and any problem allows for a wide range of solutions. It is up to you to choose the best possible option. For instance, if some team members are not generating enough sales, you may choose either to terminate those individuals or to guide and mentor them toward better results.

There are no "absolutely correct" solutions. Each solution simply needs to be correct for that particular time and in that particular context. Make sure that you determine the correct solution for your situation after weighing and exhausting every other option.

Another consideration is proportionality. The solution you propose must be proportional to the magnitude of the problem. It may be counterproductive, for example, to reevaluate your entire sales process based on problems you encounter with one individual component. Let's consider the earlier example. If one or a few team members is performing below average, it is unnecessary—and sometimes even harmful—to issue new directives to the entire team based on the actions of those few individuals. Remember, the bigger the problem, the bigger the solution and vice versa.

The nature of your solutions also depends upon the specificity of the observations. There are many different ways to define the problem and, again, no "absolutely correct" way. However, if you manage to accurately identify the root cause of the problem, you'll be better equipped to address it properly. For example, consider the following two observations: One: the number of monthly sales is dropping, and two: the number of sales is dropping because we are not properly following up with the leads and the customers.

Notice the difference? Based on the first assumption, you'd scramble to identify solutions to the dropping sales levels. You'd reevaluate the way in which you search for prospects. You'd reform the way your sales team demonstrates the product. You'd re-assess the way you close deals. You'd do so much work but see no result. On the flip side, in the second case the problem is clearly identifiable, and the solution is readily available.

IMPLEMENT

Once you know what the problem is and what the solution ought to be, the rest of the process should be easy, right? Unfortunately, you might discover that, to your dismay, this is not the case. Implementing the proposed solutions can prove to be the most difficult component of creating a process. Let us return to the example underperforming team members. You know what the problem is, and you know that termination is not the solution. What's next? What do you do to ensure that cycle doesn't continue to repeat? Think about that for a moment. If your answer is that you need to set performance indicators and constantly monitor their performance, then congratulations. You're on the right track!

Effectively implementing the proposed solutions demands constant effort and vigilance on your part. If you're not committed to bringing about results, no one else will be either. You're the captain of the ship, and you need to take control. However, recognize that once you have fully implemented the solutions, the problem may persist and/or newer problems may arise. If that occurs, you again return to the drawing board.

REVISE

Remember when I discussed the sales process as one of trial and error? Revise is the phase when that is most true. This is the phase within which you learn from your mistakes, deal with the problems created by the solutions and polish and perfect, adjust and alter, reassess and reevaluate. How does this apply to our group of unfortunately underperforming employees? At last check, you had set performance indicators to evaluate their performance. With constant monitoring and guidance, you found that most of the team members improved considerably in terms of monthly sales. A few, however, still remain behind. If all other options have been thoroughly exhausted, perhaps it would be best to allow them to pursue other interests. Perhaps car sales isn't a viable career path for them. This may be the time to hire new, more skilled and energetic team members, at which point you will notice a visible increase in monthly sales.

For the record, the process of revision and reexamination never ends. You will continue to get better and better while attempting to adapt to ever-changing circumstances. It is a constant cycle of observation, translation, implementation and revision that feeds on feedback from customers and team members alike.

6 Characteristics of a Great Sales Process

Any efficient sales process must include the following six characteristics. These are the attributes that separate the good from the bad sales processes and the factors that will determine whether your process will be a success or a failure. Let's consider them one at a time.

PREDICTABILITY

Any good sales process must produce predictable outcomes. You must be able to fairly and accurately assess the impact of your actions. If a sales process is not predictable, you're leaving results to chance, and no one wants to be in this kind of situation.

REPEATABILITY

A process, by definition, is a set of steps that is repeatable. It functions regardless of the person at the helm of the team, regardless of how many team members there are and regardless of whether they are new or experienced team members. The repeatability of the actions is what brings certainty to the mechanism as a whole. It is what enables you to achieve similar results over and over again.

ADAPTABILITY

In addition to being predictable and repeatable, a good sales process must be adaptable. It must be able to incorporate changes to meet changing circumstances, ranging from a sudden increase or decrease in walk-in customers to a shift in market conditions. Adaptable sales processes produce the best possible results at all times.

TANGIBILITY

A good sales process must be able to produce tangible results (outcomes that may be measured or quantified with a degree of certainty). For example, the number of car sales in a month can be calculated and compared at the end of each quarter in order to evaluate performance.

RELEVANCY

There are three aspects of relevancy in an efficient sales process. The process should be relevant for its time period, for you and for everyone else. It must be flexible enough to successfully navigate the various challenges encountered each day. If you are following someone else's process, you must consider whether or not it achieves the same results for your business. If it doesn't, you must amend it to suit your unique requirements. Similarly, the process you follow must be, in some way, relevant to others as well so that they, too, will benefit from it.

FLEXIBILITY

If your sales process is rigid and unyielding, it may not be right for your business. If you make changes in one component and the whole structure comes crumbling down, that is a sign that your process is in need of a major overhaul. A good sales process is flexible, and its components function somewhat independently. If you hire new employees, for example, or replace existing ones, that action must not have an impact on the nature and frequency of customer follow-ups.

An Example of Our 10-Step Sales Process

Now that we have thoroughly explored the theory and basics of how a general sales process should work, I'll introduce the specifics of the process we follow at Charles Maund, which has ten steps. The process begins with greeting a customer and ends at delivery of the purchased vehicle.

While formulating your own process, you may seek inspiration from these ten steps. You may modify some of the steps to suit your needs, or you may come up with a unique process of your own. There are no rights or wrongs; we follow the process that suits us best, and you must follow the process that suits you best.

Here are our ten steps for your consideration:

MEET AND GREET

Meet and greet is the first step. In some ways, it's one of the most crucial steps of the process, and if you don't execute this step well, you may lose the customer on the doorstep. If that happens, there's no point in proceeding to the next steps, is there? Meet and greet is, therefore, make or break. It's your chance to make a first and lasting impression. "You don't get a second chance to make a first impression," said James Uleman, a New York University psychology professor. He is absolutely correct. He can back this statement with research, and we can back it with experience.

Let's get down to brass tacks. You see a customer approaching or getting out of their car. Don't rush to him. Don't try to drag him inside. Don't start "selling" yet. Stay calm. Exude confidence. Compose yourself. Give him time to compose himself. Let him familiarize himself with the dealership. Approach him with ease and shake his hand firmly, but do not start selling. Do not start babbling about your new sales and offers and special deals and discounts. That opportunity will (hopefully) come later. Instead, simply approach him, introduce yourself, and say, "Welcome to the Dealership. May I help you find someone?" You could also ask, "How may I help you" or "Can I help you" or ask them his name. Which question you lead with doesn't matter; what matters is that you must make the customer feel at ease and not on the defensive. Your goal is to invite him in.

FACT-FINDING

Now that the customer has had a chance to familiarize himself with where he is, you need to familiarize yourself with him as well. That's where fact-finding comes in.

Fact-finding is the step in which you ask the customer a series of questions to determine what it is that he needs. "Need" is the key word here. This is absolutely crucial because there's a difference between what the customer wants and what he needs. In all my years of experience, I have seen countless customers walk in wanting, for example, a black SUV and walk out as the owners of a white sedan. Oftentimes, the disparity between what the customer thinks he wants and what he ends up buying is surprising, even to me! The point is that it is your job to ascertain not what the customer wants but what the customer needs. How do you do that? It's simple—you ask questions.

Fact-finding questions may vary considerably but the purpose is always the same. We use the following questions when we're on a fact-finding mission with a customer:

- What would you like to have if you could afford it?
- What do you have to have that you're not willing to give up?
- What features does your current car have that you don't like or that don't matter to you?
- What would you like to have next time that you don't have now?
- Are you looking for a small, mid-size or large vehicle?

- What features are must-haves for you?
- Do you want dark, medium or light colored car?
- How much do you drive per year (this question helps you assess whether or not you can get the customer into a lease if that makes more financial sense than a purchase)

The fact-finding step is essential. It is the source of your data set, and you'll find yourself coming back to the data set for reference again and again during subsequent steps. You may change the questions according to what suits you best. However, the questions must be open-ended. Notice that all of the questions begin with "what." None of them is a simple yes or no question.

Open-ended questions allow you to swiftly move from one question to the next. One thing leads to another until you find yourself immersed in a detailed conversation with the customer. This is how it should happen. Don't ask questions beginning with "do" or "does." Those questions lead only to a dead end. Once you are armed with information, you move to the next step.

VEHICLE SELECTION

No car sale is possible without a vehicle selection. What you must remember while assisting the customer with vehicle selection is that it is the customer's choice that matters, not yours. Learn to place yourself in the shoes of the customer; see the world through his eyes. This is precisely why the fact-finding step is so crucial. Remember that you are assisting the customer with what he thinks he wants, not dictating to him what he should want.

You may get increased commission on some of the slower-moving items, and that's good to know! You may attempt to push that item if it fits the customer's needs. Do not try to sell it to every customer you deal with, however. This is not the way to gain long-term customers, nor is it the way to ethically conduct business. Fall back on the fact-finding information you gathered.

Narrow down a list of vehicles that fit the requirements of the customer, and show him those vehicles. If customers want to go out of their comfort zone, it's okay, but if not, don't push your own agenda.

An important point to consider is that people are more likely to buy a car they can see, feel or touch as opposed to one they find in a brochure or online. Maintaining a healthy inventory is essential in vehicle selection. You need to walk the customer to the vehicle, let him sit in the vehicle and go on a test drive with the customer. These are important psychological factors that compel the customers to buy certain vehicles. Unless the customer has specific demands, driving a vehicle is much more convincing than reading about it in a brochure.

PRESENTATION AND DEMO

This step is the big one, and the one your sale hinges upon. This is the one step every car salesperson must know so well that he can do it in his sleep. Although we will touch upon some aspects of the presentation and demo in future chapters, it is important to discuss this part of the process here, in the context of the sales process.

A sales presentation is learned. It's an art. Just like other performing arts, it requires the unique combination of talent and hard work—but mostly hard work and, lest we forget, experience. If you are new, however, don't lose hope. You have what many other experienced sales professionals don't have—the energy, the passion and the drive to be a good salesperson. It's this energy that's infectious and convinces a customer to buy a product.

A presentation is all about balance—balance between confidence and over-confidence, energy and solemnity, being convincing and being over-bearing. If you offer too many details, the customer will lose interest. If you offer too little detail, the customer will want more. Be accurate. Be precise. Be the kind of salesperson that gets the customer in the driver's seat.

The average time for a presentation is ten minutes and involves a walk around the vehicle at which time you display the key features of the product to the customer. It is important to know everything about the vehicle but discuss only the relevant information. The walk-around can usually be broken down to six steps. These are:

1. Begin at the front of the vehicle. Explain its front features such as its aerodynamic shape.

2. Explain the key features of the engine. You can lift the hood if you'd like.

3. Move to the passenger side of the vehicle and open the doors while explaining about the side.

4. Move to the back of the vehicle and explain the rear and trunk.

5. Move to the driver's seat and open the door.

6. Seat the customer in the driver seat and explain the internal features.

If the customer asks about the details about a specific feature, you can explain more in-depth. But remember to keep the presentation to around ten minutes unless the customer shows an unusual amount of interest, and remember that the customer's interest in the product depends upon your level of enthusiasm about it. Learn to love the product, and be excited while explaining its features. If you are lively and animated, your energy will excite the customer as well. If you're dull and boring, the customer may very well lose interest.

When you are finished with the presentation, it's time for the test drive or the demo. You must remember never to ask the customer whether he would like to go on a test drive. Statistical evidence shows that almost 50 percent of customers will disagree if you ask, whereas only 30 percent will decline if you assume they want to go. The test drive is a crucial component of making up the customer's mind.

TRIAL CLOSE

This is the point when the sales process begins to enter its culminating steps. The trial close is the culmination of all of the previous steps and the beginning of the later steps. It is the bridge between an undecided mindset in the customer and the point when the customer begins to make up his mind about a particular product that he finally wants to buy.

This decision doesn't simply happen out of the blue, however. The success of the trial close step is dependent upon the incremental progress made during the earlier steps. Remember that we discussed pushing only those vehicles that customers wanted to buy? That makes the choice much narrower. Then, during the presentation, you must begin to assess whether the vehicle is actually working for the customer or not. That's not accomplished solely through observing the customer's body language and facial expressions. The presentation is not entirely a one-way communication; it can (and should) be interactive. You must begin to gather affirmative or negative signals through these interactions.

For instance, while demonstrating the seating arrangement, you might ask, "Are the seats comfortable enough for you?" or "Are you satisfied with the vehicle's safety features?" or "Are you happy with the smoothness of the ride?" Yes, yes and yes. You have three yeses—three small (but encouraging) replies. You therefore have the go-ahead to attempt the trial close.

The trial close is when you ask the real questions. These are questions that bring you and the customer closer to closing the deal, selling the car and engaging in the final handshake. Trial close questions can include, "Is this vehicle affordable for you?" or "Is it perfect for your needs?" If the answer is yes, it's time for the next step. If the answer is no, you return to the previous steps—the presentation and the demo.

TRADE-IN EVALUATION/WALK

We have traveled much further down the road to a car sale. The trade-in evaluation/walk step is the one during which tangible progress is made beyond simple discussions around the table. If the customer has comfortably entered this step, it means that he or she is fairly willing to buy the vehicle. If you play your cards right, the deal could be yours.

The trade-in step is where the customer agrees or refuses to trade in his current vehicle. If he flat-out declines to do so, there's no option other than abandoning this step and moving to the next one. However, customers often agree to a trade-in. Even if they appear slightly unwilling, remember that your display of confidence is the key. Offer to evaluate his vehicle even if he is planning to keep it. Most customers will agree to allow you to do that, even if only to see what the vehicle is worth.

The walk to the vehicle to possibly be traded in begins when you say it begins. Don't ask the customer whether or not he wants to walk. Don't wait for the customer to respond with Yes or No. Simply say something along the lines of, "Let's walk to the vehicle," and then stand up. The customer generally will follow. When you reach the vehicle, walk around it. Do a thorough (but silent) examination. Move your fingers across all the bumps, dents and scratches and ensure the customer sees you doing this.

Open the doors, and check the inside of the vehicle. Record the mileage, and visibly check the defects again before going back to the office. The confidence and authority you display during the walk makes an impression on the customer. Even if you are new, try to look like you know what you're doing. Try to take notes and look busy, and don't speak while examining the vehicle. Follow this approach, and you've done most of the work. After you do the walk, it is typically the sales manager's job to evaluate the vehicle.

WRITE UP

The write-up phase is the first step in the final negotiation process with the customer. It must begin with negotiations and end, ideally, with the customer committing to buying the vehicle. That's the salesperson's goal. You do that through a write-up, which is a document with four distinct sections (which is why it's informally known as the "foursquare write-up." Formally, it may be referred to as the "purchase order" or "customer worksheet").

The key components of a foursquare write-up are:

1. Selling price: This is the first component of the write-up—it reflects the net price of the vehicle. The salesperson should enter the full manufacturer's suggested retail price (MSRP) in the price column. Do not enter the discount price in this section, even if there is one. The negotiations must begin with the original price.

2. Trade-in value/allowance: This is the price you offer to pay to the customer for the vehicle the customer agrees to trade in. The negotiation process usually begins with the trade-in value. The customer and the salesperson will have two different values in mind. It is like a game of tug-of-war, and the goal is to pull the customer toward your value rather than the value he had in mind.

3. Down payment: This is the step where you try to discover how much cash the customer has available to pay on the day of the sale. Your objective is to secure as much of a cash-down payment as possible regardless of the equity the customer has in his trade-in.

4. Monthly payment: This is the stage where most of the negotiations occur since customers are more concerned with what they will be required to pay each month than the total price of the vehicle. This is also where the step at which

customers are most flexible since it's easier for you to increase $20 on the monthly payment than $1000 on the down payment.

NEGOTIATE AND CLOSE

After you have performed a trial close, evaluated the trade-in and worked on the write-up, it is time to engage in final negotiations and close the deal. All the preliminary steps build toward this step. How well this step goes depends entirely on how well you negotiate and close. The final negotiations are based on the four terms of sale we discussed in the write-up, and your job is to keep the negotiations as far away from the selling price as possible.

The incredibly important component of the negotiations is the "hit-figure." A hit-figure is the value that is significantly higher or lower than that which you, as the salesperson, want to settle on. For example, let's assume that the negotiations seem to center on the value of the trade-in vehicle. The customer wants to receive $10,000, and you want to settle at $8,000. You don't start the negotiations with that $8000 figure because, if you do, the figure will ultimately only increase. The hit-figure, therefore, is the artificially lowered value that you initially present to the customer to begin the negotiations. In this case, the hit-figure should be somewhere in the vicinity of $6,000. When you begin negotiations at $6,000, you will work your way up while the customer works his way down to a final agreed-to figure of $8,000.

PROPER TURN TO BUSINESS OFFICE

If you have diligently followed the above steps to reach the ninth step, congratulations! The sale is almost complete. The only thing you need to do now is to secure the necessary documentations and go through the formal sales procedures, which is accomplished through a trip to the business office. The business office may also be referred to as Finance and Insurance (F&I). It is the place where the finance person formally secures the car deal, assists with a smooth transition of the vehicle from the dealership to the customer and helps the customer secure financing for the deal.

Some of the documentation that the business office works on includes lender contracts, powers of attorney and title work documents. Other documents intended to secure more of the customer's investment may include insurance programs and extended service agreements. The business office also helps customers with their customer statements or credit applications.

It is imperative to note that this is merely an overview of what the business office *might* do. As a salesperson, you must not mention all potential offers to the customers right off the bat. What you offer the customer depends upon the rules of your specific dealership. Your job is simply to introduce the customer to the finance officer, and he or she will take it from there.

DELIVERY

You are a salesperson. You delivered the presentation. You negotiated with the customer. You closed the deal. You referred the customer to the finance department. Therefore, your job is naturally over, right? Well, not quite.

A good salesperson's job is to work in the interest of the customer and the interest of the dealership at the same time. An improper delivery process leads to a customer's dissatisfaction and, in turn, a drop in the dealership's customer satisfaction ratings.

If you don't deliver the vehicle properly, you fail on both counts. You need to play an active role in the delivery process—even if your dealership has a dedicated delivery coordinator.

In order to ensure a smooth delivery, you must work off of a delivery checklist for the vehicle, which is typically developed by the dealership or the manufacturer. You need to inspect the vehicle yourself—not as a salesperson but, instead, as if you are the customer. You need to see the vehicle through the customer's eyes. Make sure the vehicle is clean and does not have any defects. Make sure the gas tank is full when the vehicle leaves the dealership. Make sure all the additional after-market equipment the customer ordered is in place and in optimal condition. While the customer is busy in the business office, you must work on every aspect of the delivery process before handing over the car keys to the customer.

You now have a brief overview of both a general and a particular process. It's time to move to the next stage of the sales procedure: Salesmanship.

Salesmanship

Salesmanship is probably the most integral component of the sales procedure. If you don't have good salesmanship skills, you cannot even begin to imagine selling a single car a month, let alone 1000.

Any delicious meal requires top-quality ingredients and a well-crafted recipe. A sumptuous steak needs the right cut of beef and the right chef to prepare it with great care. Good beef, cooked to perfection, makes a steaming hot, tender, juicy steak. Is this description making your mouth water? What if I presented you with a bland, overcooked, tough steak that you couldn't chew? Does that sound appetizing? It doesn't to me.

A car sales procedure is similar to cooking a fine steak. It requires the proper ingredients; the ingredients of a sales procedure are the salespeople. The right sales team can work wonders, and if you don't have a good team, you won't sell as many vehicles as you want no matter how hard you try as a manager or team member. Just as good meals require a skilled chef, the sales procedure requires the proper use of salesmanship tips, tricks and techniques. There you have it—a magnificent sales procedure presented to you on a plate.

UNDERSTANDING YOUR SCOPE OF SALES

When it comes to salesmanship, we also need to consider the width of its scope. Gary Keller's book, *The Millionaire Real Estate Agent*, perfectly addresses this concept. In it, Keller talks about the importance of focusing on not only one avenue of sales but instead on a little bit of everything. If I break it down through a salesperson's perspective, it goes like this: You must focus on selling to at least five customers in each of the following five categories: internet, chat, phone, floor, referrals and prospecting.

You must also constantly push further each and every day in order to meet that goal through your actions. This is how some of the most successful 30-cars-per-month salespeople (including myself) make sales—by increasing our actions with every opportunity. If it required 25 calls of prospecting to make one appointment, then in order to make 10 appointments we needed to make a total of 250 calls! This is the kind of thinking you must instill in your staff. The more you push them to go from good to great, the sooner you can take them to the next level. Your follow-up must be relentless.

6 Critical Salesmanship Skills

Great salesmanship requires a unique combination of skills and techniques. Most of these skills are naturally associated with your personality traits. If you have great social skills and are naturally affable and amiable, you will have an advantage. There is such a thing as being a born salesman, but don't be disappointed if you aren't one. Skills can be learned through hard work and practice, and acquired skills are as valuable—perhaps even more so—than natural skills. If you have what it takes to be a salesman, you must channel your abilities in a specific direction.

Following are some of the skills required to be a great salesperson:

UNDERSTAND THE CUSTOMER

An effective and ethical sales process is all about satisfying the needs of the customer while simultaneously generating profit for your organization. How can you satisfy the customer, however, if you don't understand him? Direct all of your initial energy toward getting an idea of what exactly the customer wants. Listening is key. Listen. Absorb. Analyze. Actively listen to the "what" that the customer is trying to convey. Absorb the information, and make it your mantra throughout your interactions with the customer. Analyze every aspect of what the customer requires and how you can translate the demands of the customer into profit for your organization.

It is also vital to understand without having an agenda. As a car salesperson, you will be given specific targets by management. You may be required to push certain vehicles over others. That's your agenda. When the customer leaves home to buy a vehicle, however, he has certain features in mind. That's his agenda. Whose agenda should ultimately prevail? Obviously, the customer's. The customer is the most important person, and your job is to assist him with what he wants to buy and what's best for his particular needs. It is not your job to dictate to the customer what he should buy.

Some customers are not naturally expressive or articulate enough to be able to convey exactly what they want. In that case, it's your job to extract the information out of them with ease. Be interested. Be inquisitive. Ask great questions. The goal is to ease the customer into a frank conversation about what he wants. Some customers will get to the point straight away; others will hesitate or expect you to magically lead them to the perfect vehicle. Asking questions will help you with some of the more difficult customers. But be careful not to be overbearing. The customer should not feel as though he is being interviewed. Let him know that you are asking these questions in order to be able to help him find the right vehicle.

You may be wondering about what specific questions you should ask. Don't worry; there is a set of questions to lead you in the right direction, and these questions may be dealership-related, vehicle-related, trade-in-related or budget-related.

Dealership-related questions help you inquire about the customer's previous experience with other dealerships and/or why they chose your dealership. Ask if yours is the first dealership they chose. Ask if they came in because of a specific vehicle the dealership is advertising. Ask if they knew about a specific sale or event the dealership is having that day. Vehicle-related questions help you determine which kind of vehicle will best suit the customer's needs. You can inquire about some of the features the customer wants in a vehicle, or the customer's preferences while looking for a new vehicle. Some might prefer safety features while others might be more interested in mileage options. It is also important to ask about the customer's budget range and whether or not they have a vehicle to trade in.

BE SOCIABLE AND EASY-GOING

Have you ever met a successful salesperson who is discourteous, unapproachable, cold or unkind? I bet not. Because they don't exist.

You may be a salesperson with any or all of the aforementioned negative attributes but you won't be one for very long, and you certainly won't be successful. To be a good salesperson, you must appear friendly and easy-going. You must have great social skills. This doesn't mean that you need to be a life-of-the-party kind of person. Sociability, in the context of car sales, simply means that you can get along well with new people. You must be able to deal with all kinds of people. And, above all, you must show the customers the respect that they deserve. Sociability goes a long way; it creates a positive impact on the customer and substantially increases the potential for a successful sale.

Empathy is a prerequisite to sociability in salesmanship. You must be able to empathize with your customer. Think of every sale as a potential problem that the customer has. Customers come to you with their problem, and it's your job to find a solution. For example, a customer may have the problem that he wants to buy a vehicle that gives him excellent gas mileage at an affordable price. In this case, you put yourself in the customer's shoes; if you were the customer and had a wide range of options from which to choose in a particular price range, which option would you select? This is the way that your thought process must operate. Don't, however, get lost in thought as soon as the customer asks a question—that creates brooding salespeople and distraught customers. The answers must be at your fingertips.

What if you are more of an introvert or a generally quiet person? Does this type of personality doom your sales process from the beginning? Not necessarily. Sociability is, in life, an attribute. In sales, however, it is an art. Just like any other art, it can be honed through dedication to the craft and constant practice. It involves a repeatable series of actions: greet the customer, ask the questions, demonstrate the vehicle, employ humor and be courteous. You must learn these actions and be able to go with the flow.

Think about it: how many singers, comedians, actors or performance artists have you seen who are *bombtastic* on stage but shy in real life? There's a marked difference between the way a performer acts on stage and the way he acts in real life. This is because what they do on stage— whether singing or dancing or anything else—is rehearsed. They spend years in perfecting their skills and craft. Selling cars—selling anything—is similar. If you aren't naturally outgoing, you put on a performance by going through the motions—just without the funny dresses.

HAVE GREAT PRESENTATION SKILLS

While we are on the subject of performance, what better skill to discuss than presentation? After all, presentation is just another word for performance. Sociability and presentation go hand-in-hand and, therefore, share similar requirements. Just as sociability can be acquired, presentation skills can be learned as well. They are two faces of a single coin, two aspects of the same skill: effective communication. In the earlier steps of the sales process, you are the listener and the customer is, in a way, the presenter. Your role was passive. But then it changes. You become the presenter, and the customer becomes the listener.

There's a key difference between the customer and you in the Presenter role. When the customer is speaking, you don't have any choice but to listen. When you are speaking, however, the customer has a choice not to listen. That's why you need to be captivating and say the right things, the things the customer wants to hear. How do you know what it is the customer wants to hear? To know the answer, you must go back to your understanding of the customer. So you see, all of the steps interlink. One step leads to another (and sometimes back to a previous one). One skill enhances another.

Let's assume you know exactly what the customer wants. And he wants a vehicle that is economic as well as luxurious. You have that information, and you use it to the advantage of both the customer and yourself. You demonstrate how comfortable the seats are and how lavish the car's interior is. Knowing what the customer wants is necessary in order to give a skilled presentation. Knowing what the customer wants is necessary in order to give a skilled presentation.

Like any good performance, the presentation must be rehearsed. Earlier, we described what a car walk-around looks like. Learn it. Memorize it. Internalize it. A good presentation appears instinctive. You know exactly what to do every step of the way. Experience also plays a role in a good presentation and, therefore, more experienced salespeople are also often more skilled presenters. If you are a new salesperson, you will undoubtedly need practice. Stand in front of a mirror and deliver your presentation. Better yet, record yourself while presenting. It may be hard to watch at first but, with time, your style and confidence will fall into place.

LEARN TO LOVE THE PRODUCT

During the course of your sales career, you may come to realize that you have great social and presentation skills but still aren't able to do as well as some of the other salespeople. The customers are simply not as enthusiastic as you need them to be. They are not willing to buy from you, and something seems to be lacking. You don't seem to have the vigor, the energy, or the oomph that sales require. It may be that you don't love the product. How can the customer be excited about a product that you yourself aren't excited about? And how can you be excited about something you don't love?

You love the job, and you love working in sales, but you just don't love the product you're selling. If that's the case, it's time to learn a valuable lesson. If you want to succeed, you need to learn to love the product you're selling.

The key word here is "learn." Not everyone is lucky enough to sell what he inherently loves. When you enter the automobile industry, you might not love cars. You might not even know enough about cars to sell them. I understand that. I understand it because I didn't love cars when I started off. In fact, I didn't ever consider car sales as a career option. Circumstances pushed me toward this career. But I survived and, in fact, I thrived. I was successful due to many factors, but not the least among them was that I learned to love my job. I learned to love the products I sold. I learned. That's the bottom line.

KNOW EVERYTHING ABOUT THE PRODUCT

When you love something or someone, you want to know everything about them. And when you know so much about them, you want to show the world what you know. It's a common instinct. Nowhere is this instinct more valuable than in sales. In sales, you must know what you sell and sell what you know. Knowledge is power; knowledge is everything. And there's no such thing as knowing too much. A good salesman is one who knows everything about the product and is able to demonstrate a good chunk of that knowledge in an impressive manner. But it's not always as easy as it may sound.

There are various aspects of product knowledge in car sales. First, you need to know everything about the vehicle itself. In today's world, it is fairly easy for the average customer to go online and find out all they need to know about the vehicle they want to buy. All the information in the world is merely a few clicks away. These customers don't really need a salesperson who offers them half-baked or generalized information; they need a walking, talking database that can answer each and every question they have. Therefore, knowing everything is not just an advantage; it's a requirement. Second, you need to stay up-to-date when it comes to newer models and features. Remember, you must stay one step ahead of the customers.

It's one thing to know everything about a product and another thing to be able to find ways to demonstrate that knowledge. I have seen many young and energetic salespeople try to display their extensive knowledge about a vehicle in order to win over customers.

This exercise usually includes the use of technical terminology as well as long, tedious and exhaustive presentations. Well-intentioned though it may be, this is the wrong approach. What you must do is filter out all irrelevant information and focus only on those aspects of the vehicle that the customer is interested in. Any successful demonstration requires a precarious balance between how much you know and how much you show.

The aforementioned advice works for salespeople with little-to-no experience. If, however, you are a manager or a team leader, it's likely safe to assume that product knowledge isn't a problem for you. Why, then, should product knowledge be an area of concern? Here's why: as a team leader, it is your responsibility to ensure that the team members are all on the same level where product knowledge is concerned. If any one of them lags behind, he or she pulls the whole team down, and you don't want that. You must, therefore, organize frequent training sessions that cover the basics of the required-to-know information of about each vehicle. Apart from that, you must constantly push your team members to learn more and more about what they are selling. Only by being a proactive leader can you ensure that your team gets exactly where you want it to get—and stays there.

LEARN TO DEAL WITH DIFFERENT KINDS OF CUSTOMERS

It goes without saying that any successful salesperson must know how to deal with different personalities. In sales, you get the good with the bad; some customers are easy to work with while others present a challenge. Some are naturally expressive while others are shy or hesitant. Some value knowledge while others value sociability. Customers won't change their personalities for you, so it is up to you to mold your approach according to their expectations, to act and think in the way that they prefer. That's a key component to selling more cars—learning manage with different types of customers.

What exactly are the different types of customers you may encounter? Are there any specific personality traits you need to look for? What are the various ways to deal with different personality types? Classifying human beings on the basis of personalities is a complex task and one that's best left to psychologists. That said, a basic understanding of human psychology is required in sales, and it's therefore helpful to have a general idea of the kinds of customers you may encounter. The classification we have found to be the most effective was first introduced to me by R.C. Evans. According to Evans, there are four customer types:

<u>Dominant/Driver:</u> This is the type of person who likes to take control and feel in charge. During your dealings with these customers, this customer will attempt to direct the flow of conversation. He will be demanding and know exactly what he wants, when he wants it and how he wants it. In extreme situations, this personality type may be intimidating, but it's important not to back down when interacting with them. When working with them, you must act like them. If they know exactly what they want, you should know exactly what to give them. If they are authoritative in their decision-making, you must be confident in your abilities as well.

<u>Egoist/Expressive:</u> The name says it all. The defining feature of someone with an egoist personality is generally the most advantageous factor for you when negotiating: his ego. If you want to close sales with an egoist/expressive personality, you must stroke his ego. Complement him on his decisiveness. Praise his choice. Admire his insights and knowledge of the product. Remember not to overdo it,

however, and to be subtle. If you can execute properly, the deal is in your pocket.

Complacent/Amiable: This personality type is usually the easiest to work with. This person is friendly and relatable. Since his or her approach to buying is unique, your approach to selling them must also be unique. Connect with this customer, not as a businessman but as a human being. With this customer, it's not about the product; it's about the relationship. You're not selling a vehicle; you're selling yourself. Make an extra effort to remember these customers' names, and try to make their shopping experience more fun.

Stable/Analytical: This personality type is systematic. This customer prefers to analyze each and every consequence of his actions, and you should learn to recognize that quality. If the customer is organized, you must be methodical. The best way to close the deal with this customer is the method of contrast: pros and cons, advantages and disadvantages, benefits and drawbacks. It's better to use a visual approach. Make a list of pros and cons as well as a list all advantages and disadvantages to buying a particular vehicle. With regard to the specific vehicle you wish to sell him, make the list of pros considerably heavier than the list of cons. If you play your cards right and argue your point well, you'll be on your way to success.

FOCUS ON YOUR GOALS

Goals, targets, and objectives—what would we do without them? Philosophers may dwell on the eternal mysteries of why we are each in the world and yet consistently fail to find an answer. But we know exactly why salespeople are here.

We are here to achieve goals, and that's why we need a process. That's why we need salesmanship. The only reason you chose to read this book is to find out how to sell 1000 cars per month, which is, in and of itself, a goal. Sales is a constant process of setting targets for yourself and then finding various different ways to achieve them. If you're not focused on that, you're not a good salesperson.

Success in sales comes from setting the right goals and then focusing on how to attain them. In our case, we need to sell 1000 cars per month. That's our objective. The 10-step process is the means by which we do that. Therefore, we have the means, and we have a goal. Do we have everything we need? No. One key element is missing, and that is the determination to use those means to achieve the goal.

This raises even more practical questions. How exactly do we set our targets? How do we go about achieving them? Fortunately, I have already established both your target and your process. Therefore, as a salesperson, figuring out those two components isn't your concern. What must concern you, however, is the importance of focusing on goals in salesmanship. You don't do that by constantly thinking about how good your life will be once you achieve them; you do it by increasing activity.

There are different ways the management and the sales team might go about focusing on the dealership's goals. The management's job is to set the KPIs and measure employees' performance against those indicators. That way, they can keep the team focused on the right goals and know if any one of the team members deviates from them. Daily targets can be particularly beneficial.

For example, as I mentioned earlier, we follow the 4-3-2-1 rule. In a particular day, a single team member must deal with a minimum of 4 customers, go on 3 test drives, perform 2 write-ups and close 1 sale. That's a significant goal against which we measure employee performance.

The 4-3-2-1 rule makes it is easier for us to measure performance against a set standard. It also enables us to face daily challenges in a much more efficient manner. For example, if a salesperson is not meeting four customers in a day, we have ourselves a problem, and we need to examine that problem in order to come up with a solution. We must ask, "Why is he not meeting four customers? Does the problem lie in the way he greets the customers? Or are there simply not enough customers for him to engage?" When we accurately pinpoint the problem, it becomes easier to find a solution. In this case, we might resolve the problem by improving the way the salespeople meet and greet, or devise methods to increase the number of walk-in customers in any given day.

HANDLE OBJECTIONS AND QUESTIONS LIKE A PRO

In sales, every question is a challenge and every objection is an opportunity. How well you deal with customers' questions and objections determines how successful you will be in closing deals. There are two requirements when efficiently handling questions and objections. First, you need to hold your ground and be confident and firm in your response. Second, you need to be flexible and knowledgeable enough to properly satisfy the customer. More importantly, you need to avoid some of the common mistakes salespeople make while addressing questions and objections.

If a customer asks a question or raises an objection, you must:

1. **Listen:** This goes back to understanding the desires and demands of the customer. Just as you must actively listen to a customer says he wants, you also must have a good ear for the kind of questions he asks and the objections he raises. Sometimes, these slight detours will offer valuable insight into the customer's mindset and enlighten you with regard to what they really want. Sometimes, the objections can lead you into entirely new territories in which you realize that the car you were trying to sell them was not a good fit for their needs after all, and a different car might be the better one for them. If you don't truly listen to the objection, however, you will likely miss an opportunity.

2. **Explore:** Once you pay much-needed attention to the customer's question or concern, you may want to further explore it in order to properly address it. There are several ways to go about this task. You might attempt to restate the question by paraphrasing it. This approach buys you time to think about an actual response while showing the customer that you really care about his concerns. The restatement begins with, "Do I understand you correctly?" Keep in mind that this might not work for simple questions or observations. In those cases, you must explore by asking more specific questions.

3. **Address:** This is the most important aspect of the entire exercise. The customer raised the objection in order for it to be addressed, and you listened carefully and explored it so that you could better address it. This is the time for action. If you know the answer, provide an in-depth response that addresses all the aspects of the customer's concern. But what if you don't know the answer to the customer's

question? Don't worry; none of us can know everything! If you don't know the answer to a question, simply and honestly let the customer know that. Apologize, take note of the question, and don't forget to address it later. You can write it down and reassure the customer that you will get back to him.

4. **Move on:** Once you've answered the question or addressed the objection, it is important not to be-come bogged down by the details. You must swiftly move on with the process.

Helpful Salesmanship Techniques

"Salesmanship, too, is an art; the perfection of its technique requires study and practice," said James Cash Penney, the founder of JC Penney stores. Study and practice are the actions to be stressed. You must read up on common salesmanship techniques and implement those in daily practice. It's a constant implementation of both theory and practice. Once you develop all of the skills required to be a good salesperson, you need to channel those skills through your salesmanship techniques. Here's an overview of some of the sales techniques that we've found helpful in our journey:

PRE-PLAN, PRACTICE, PERFECT, PERFORM

Tom Hopkins, author of *How to Master the Art of Selling*, has a set of sales techniques that will help you not only achieve your targets but also in increasing the number of deals you successfully close. Enthusiasm, claims Hopkins, is the greatest closing tool of all. If you don't have enthusiasm for what you do, you can never be as successful as some of the other salespeople around you.

In order to build that enthusiasm, he presents the four P's: Pre-plan, Practice, Perfect and Perform. Let's see what impact these techniques have on the art of successfully selling cars.

1. **Pre-plan:** This technique works regardless of whether you are a sales manager or a team member; whether you are presenting, meeting new clients, demonstrating a vehicle, searching for prospects or following up with customers; regardless of the industry you belong to. It just works, period. The importance of planning in increasing sales cannot be stressed enough. The planning might include the creation of a formal monthly or quarterly sales plan or simply planning the day's activities beforehand. This is the one activity that separates professionals from the rest. Professionals plan. They organize. They know exactly what they need, and do exactly what's required to achieve it.

2. **Practice:** Once you have formulated the plan, once you know what to do to achieve your targets, you practice. You practice the meet and greet. You practice the demonstration. You practice the walk-around and evaluation. You practice each and every step of the sales process in order to hone it, shape it and perfect it. Hopkins doesn't believe that practice makes perfect. Practice is critical, but you must practice what works and abandon what does not. Therefore, perfect practice makes perfect. Don't waste time practicing with tools that don't work and methods that don't produce results. The results are what matters, and you only practice that which brings you closer to your goal.

3. **Perfect:** You only practice to perfect your craft. Otherwise, what's the point? Half-baked sales strategies don't

work. You must be the best in the world at what you do. Perfection comes with experience, so don't fret when you make mistakes. Don't be discouraged by poor performance. If you do, it will be the end of your career. Instead, strive toward betterment every single day. Find ways to improve, advance and act on them. That's how you perfect.

4. **Perform:** We discussed earlier that sales has much in common with performance arts. When you sell, you perform. According to Hopkins, "You are putting on a performance with every client contact. This doesn't mean you are phony. It means you are saying the right words the right way to get the end result that is in the best interest of your clients." Another aspect of performance is that, since you're putting on an act, it doesn't matter what kind of person you are or what kind of mood you're in on any given day. What matters is whether or not you perform well.

---

10 Common Sales Mistakes

Now that we know some of the common sales skills and techniques, let's look at some of the common mistakes salespeople make. It's essential to identify these mistakes and avoid them like the plague from the very beginning. You don't need to spend years trying to identify these mistakes yourself because I've narrowed down the Top 10 Frequent Mistakes that hold salespeople back.

NOT ASKING QUALIFYING QUESTIONS

Some salespeople, in their haste to start selling the product, forget to ask questions to qualify the customer before they begin. Others hesitate to ask these critical questions. And others don't think it's important enough to ask these questions. Asking questions to qualify the customer helps determine whether or not the prospective buyer is a fit for the sale.

The traditional view of qualifying the customer is simple— or, should we say, simplistic. In this context, "qualifying" refers to simply determining whether or not the customer can afford the vehicle. Qualifying can mean more than that, however.

Qualifying includes not simply assessing the customer's financial capability but also the exact nature of his demands. The salesperson must begin by asking questions to determine:

- Whether the customer can afford the vehicle
- The kind of vehicle the customer is looking for
- The features the customer is looking for in a vehicle

STARTING TO SELL RIGHT AWAY

"Hello and welcome to the XYZ dealership. Are you looking for a vehicle? We have an excellent sale today and a wide range of vehicles for you to choose from. Step right in to the best dealership in town." Stop it right there!

Let's begin again. First, relax a bit. This is one of the biggest mistakes that car salespeople make—they jump straight to the sale. The sleazy salesman method doesn't work anymore. In fact, it can even be counterproductive in some cases. Don't start selling right away. Don't even approach the customer sooner than he would like. Give the customer time to breathe, take-in his surroundings and adjust to the environment before approaching him.

Once you approach, do so with an intention of establishing a relationship. Ask the customer's name, and offer him your name. Welcome him to the dealership. Be friendly and courteous. Once he's fully adjusted to the environment, start with the qualifying questions, not the sales pitch itself.

OFFERING TOO MUCH OR TOO LITTLE INFORMATION

These are two extremes that must be avoided at all times. If you provide too little information, you leave your customers wanting more. If you provide too much information, customers are confused. You have to be careful about how to convey product knowledge. I have stressed this again and again because it's so important, yet few sales people realize that they're doing it incorrectly.

You don't need to be dishonest to the customer and/or conceal crucial information. You need to find a way to convey relevant information in fewer words. "Brevity," according to Shakespeare, "is the soul of wit." This principle works in car sales as much as in literature. Learn to constantly tweak your presentation, remove what's unnecessary, add what's been left out and keep it somewhere around 10 minutes.

Another mistake salespeople often commit is trying to use technical jargon and complex words in attempt to impress the customer. Don't do that. Customers have incredibly short attention spans. Taking this approach makes it likely that they'll lose the thread and you'll lose a sale.

CONSTANTLY TALKING

In order to properly make this point, a few flawed assumptions about sales need to be addressed.

First, it is not the obligation of the salesperson to fill in silences by constantly talking about how great the products and services are. Some salespeople continue to talk far beyond convincing the customer without even realizing it. By continuing to talk way past the sell, they risk losing the customer altogether.

Second, a sales presentation is not a one-way communication. In fact, it's the exact opposite. It's a two-way communication even though primarily one person does the talking. You must learn to read the expressions and body language of the customer. Is she bored? Is she enthusiastic? Is she convinced? If you cannot get a read on the customer, it doesn't hurt to simply ask questions. This leads us to the third point.

Not asking for the close early enough is one of the biggest mistakes that salespeople make.

DISCUSSING PRICE AFTER PRESENTATION

Imagine spending 10 minutes of both your and the customer's valuable time demonstrating the vehicle. You're quite proud of how well it went, and the customer seems happy, too. All is well. That is, until price comes up.

The vehicle ends up being way beyond the customer's price range. All your efforts are wasted, and you need to start again. It's a frustrating situation to be in, but it can be avoided if you simply discuss the price before you begin the presentation.

Most customers make up their minds regarding the amount of money they want to spend on a vehicle before even arriving at the dealership. Do not hesitate to discuss the customer's preferred price range before you proceed. The best time to do that is through qualifying questions. Discussing price also narrows down the range of vehicles that might suit best the customer.

SELLING TO ONLY ONE PERSON

Most customers don't arrive at the dealership alone, however one of them is typically the key decision-maker while the other members of the group are merely influencers. The mistake salespeople often commit is, they entirely rule out the role of the influencer and deal only with the decision-maker. It is crucial to avoid this error at all costs. By ignoring the influencers, you're letting go of a potential advantage in closing the deal. Influencers often play a critical role in convincing the key decision-makers.

While it's more convenient to deal with a single person during negotiations, it's important not to ignore the influencers while presenting information or conducting a demonstration. Sell to everyone. Something that doesn't click with the decision-maker may convince the influencer enough to shift the deal in your favor. If your customers are a married couple, pay attention to the preferences of both and try to sell to the wife in addition to the husband.

IGNORING WHAT THE CUSTOMER WANTS

If you choose to do this, don't even bother trying to close the deal. You're fighting a lost cause already. The customer is important; he isn't just a series of numbers. He's not a walking target. Sam Walton summed it up perfectly when he said, "There is only one boss. The customer. And he can fire everybody in the company from the chairman on down, simply by spending his money somewhere else." If you are intent on ignoring the customer's desires, you might as well start looking for new career options immediately.

It's important not only to listen to what customer says but also take note of the visual cues he throws your way. If the customer is not generally responsive, you should actively try to ask questions to get his feedback every step of the way. And if he asks a question or raises an objection, devote all your energy toward addressing the concerns without overdoing it. Dealing with the customer is not an easy task. You must tread carefully.

HOUNDING THE CUSTOMERS

This is a common mistake made by salespeople who don't value listening to the customer. Yes, salesmanship does require a degree of hunger to close. You don't, however, have to be aggressive. Even if you succeed in bullying the customers enough that they buy the product, you've made a sale but likely eliminated the possibility of 10 future sales. Aggressive sales strategies may work in door-to-door marketing but not in established businesses like car dealerships that rely on repeat clients and good word-of-mouth.

Surprisingly, car sales is one of the industries in which bullying techniques occur most often. Salespeople employ all possible means to get customers to buy the most expensive cars so that they can rake in the highest commissions. This is why car salespeople generally have such a bad reputation. These strategies may do wonders in achieving the sales targets for the first couple of months, but in the longer run they do more harm than good.

IGNORING THE FOLLOW-UP

The follow-up in car sales is one of the four integral steps of the sales process. It's so essential that I have dedicated an entire chapter to its importance. You must never ignore the follow-up. If the customer asked you to give them a few days to think things over and you forgot to call or keep in touch through email, you've just lost a potentially valuable sale as well as any prospects for future sales or referrals. For every customer you don't follow up with, you lose 10 potential sales.

A good follow-up is required even after you close the deal, and it benefits you as a salesperson as well as the dealership. This is the step that turns a one-time customer into a repeat customer, and repeat customers are key to the success of your business.

NOT SEEKING OUT NEWER CLIENTS

If you have worked hard and followed everything in this book diligently and sold 1000 cars in a month, you've achieved everything, right? You're at the top of the ladder, and there's nowhere to go, right? That couldn't be further from the truth.

Once you break the thousand-car mark, the real challenge begins. Your goal is not just to sell 1000 cars in a given month; your goal is to sustain sales at that level and eventually surpass it.

This cannot be achieved without seeking newer clients. Simply regularly following up with previous clients isn't enough, even if you are the most successful dealership in town or have good word-of-mouth. You must always go one step further. You must always actively seek out new business. If you don't do that, your success might crumble until you're desperately struggling to find new clients. So why not do it earlier?

Closing the Sale

When it comes to car sales, selling is closing and closing is selling. That's the bottom line. Even if you took the steps to meticulously craft a sales process, even if you hired the best sales team available, even if you developed the skills and perfected the techniques required to boost monthly sales, all of your efforts could go down in flames if you don't know how to close the deal. As Alec Baldwin stated in his famous speech in the film Glengarry Glen Ross, only three things matter in sales: ABC. "A=always B=be C=closing. Always Be Closing. Always be closing!"

The closing of the sale is more important than the quality of the product. It's more crucial than the efficacy of your marketing strategy. It's more difficult than the rest of the process put together. Yet if you have successfully established a relationship with the customer, you may find it easier than eating a piece of cake. The key here, as it is in every other aspect of sales, is to work hard. Spend valuable time and energy on your closing pitch. Practice. Rehearse. Train.

Many factors contribute to how well you're able to close a deal. Some of these factors include experience, training, hard work, persistence, persuasiveness, charm, skill and sheer dumb luck.

WHAT DO I MEAN WHEN I SAY "CLOSE?"

Close the deal, close the sale, close the customer. These kinds of phrases are casually thrown around in the world of sales. Everyone is in pursuit to unlock a golden tablet or map that will help him close more often and more successfully. However, few pay much attention to what closing really signifies. If we can better understand the meaning of the word "close," we can better determine how to do it more effectively.

Closing (in sales) refers to the action whereby you transform a prospective buyer into a customer. It's the final step in any financial transaction. It's the point at which you sell a product in exchange for money, and it's the ultimate goal of every salesperson. Not all closing moments are successful, however. In this moment, the customer either finally agrees to buy, or he decides that your product or service is not worth his valuable money.

Rejection—no matter how experienced you are—can be tough. What's most important, however, is how well you can get back up and push forward.

Although it takes great effort to bring customers to the point where you can close the deal, it takes even greater skill to get them to utter the final yes. It's a skill that may be considered, at best, artful and, at worst, conning. Many businesses hire qualified people specifically for this job. Many assign this task to their most experienced professionals, and these individuals are known as the "closers." Their job is to ensure that customers don't leave without buying.

Salesmanship and the Art of Closing

I f there's one basic indicator that's best used to evaluate a salesperson's performance, it is his or her ability to close. How many cars did he sell in a month? The formula seems simple. The more cars you sell, the better salesperson you are. But it isn't quite that simple. Various other indicators are important as well and must be considered.

How well does a particular salesperson greet a customer? How well does he present and demonstrate? How personable and charming is he? All of these qualities must be considered. In the end, however, what it boils down to is: can a particular salesperson sell enough cars, and does he know how to close?

In addition to knowing how to close, it's important to know *when* to close. Most inexperienced salespeople go for the close either too early or too late. It's important to find that brief window in which you can seize the golden opportunity. Knowing when that window has appeared depends upon two things: the nature of your relationship with the customer and the level of communication with the customer. The former dictates whether the customer feels comfortable enough with you to agree to the sale earlier than usual. The latter determines whether or not you can accurately assess if the customer is willing to buy at any given time.

THE CHANGING VIEW OF CLOSING

"In the rush to close deals, we too often forget the human factor and squander the long-term opportunity," says Jeff Thull, author of *Mastering The Complex Sale*. "We need to address the hopes, fears and aspirations of our customers and create mutually beneficial relationships." In a small number of words, Thull has beautifully illustrated the changing view of the sales community as a whole on closing deals.

The old view of closing in sales was that all prospective buyers had cash in their pockets and businesses had products to sell. The job of the salesperson was to sell as many products as possible to earn as much cash as possible by closing as many deals as possible. This is an utterly unsophisticated and somewhat overly simplistic outlook on the sales process, and it is now obsolete. In fact, many successful businesses and large corporations are moving away from this traditionalist approach because it simply no longer works.

There are many reasons why a shift away from the traditional approach is necessary. If businesses sell simply for the sake of making a sale in order to earn money, it leaves the customer unsatisfied because he believes that, somehow, he has been shortchanged. As a result, he doesn't buy again. And when businesses don't get return clients, they run out of steam.

Today's customers are smart, observant and adept. They deserve our attention, and they deserve to be treated as human beings, not just walking targets. The first rule of business is, the customer is important. This rule was not born out of merely an altruistic sense of public service. It has practical consequences. When you close, you must do it in such a way that the customer not only comes back to you but also contributes to a significant increase in sales through referrals. Therefore, you have two options: adopt this approach or go out of business. The choice is yours.

Common Closing Techniques

Before reading further, ask yourself this question: why do you want to learn about common closing techniques? Are you looking for a one-size-fits-all solution that will help you magically close more deals and make you top salesperson overnight? If so, you can stop reading further because all the knowledge in the world cannot create that kind of magic. Closing deals cannot be achieved solely by using any or all of these techniques. In addition, patience, wit, personality and tact are required. Closing a sale does not depend solely or tricks and/or tips. If it did, you would not need the information contained within this book!

It is important to learn about closing techniques, how to define what a closing technique is, and which techniques should be used and when.

Let's first break down the term "closing techniques." It's made up of two words: *closing* and *techniques*. If you have read this far, you are be fully aware of the meaning of the word "closing." Technique, on the other hand, can be defined in many ways: a skill, a method, a procedure. My favorite definition identifies technique as "the manner and ability with which an artist, writer, dancer, athlete or the like employs the technical skills of a particular art or field of endeavor."

Sales is an art, which you've likely heard countless times. Therefore, salespeople are artists. As such, any closing technique is a manner in which we employ the technical skills of our particular field.

Two words deserve our attention at this point: manner and skills. We had an extensive discussion about salesmanship skills in the previous chapter. If you have brought the customer to the point where you're going fin or the close, it may be safely assumed that you possess at least a few of the salesmanship skills we've discussed. The manner that you employ is the defined way in which you utilize those skills. A closing technique can, therefore, be described simply as the manner in which you apply your sales skill in order to close a deal.

This still leaves the questions Why, Which and When. Why should we learn about closing techniques? Which techniques should we use? When should we use them? I mentioned earlier that there is no one technique that is a panacea for all sales-related ills. However, many salespeople looking for shortcuts already know that, so they try to use these techniques randomly. It's like throwing a bunch of darts at a board and hoping that one of them sticks. But customers are smart, and they see right through that approach. They can sense how desperate the salesperson is, and this gives them leverage during negotiations. So, in this case, the techniques you depended on backfired miserably. It's helpful to know when to use a particular technique.

The type of technique you employ at any given time, and with any given customer, depends upon your ability to understand that customer. Do you possess the most important salesmanship skill? Can you understand your customers? Can you work with different types of people? If so, you will know which technique to use when.

These are some of the most common closing techniques:

OPINION CLOSE

This is the most straightforward closing technique. In an opinion close, all you have to do is directly ask the customer about hurdles to closing the deal. For instance, you presented and demonstrated a car that the customer seems to like. However, he or she still seems hesitant to giving you the final yes. Something is holding him back; you can see it. Something is stopping him from commit-ting to the sale. Why not just ask him directly, "Is there anything holding you back from saying yes?" Perhaps he'll say the issue is price. The deal is not yet closed, but at least you have something definitive to go on; you know what you need to do in order to close the deal.

An opinion close may not seal the deal for you then and there, but it opens newer avenues. For example, a discussion on price may lead the customer to increase his buying range or see another vehicle that better matches his preferred price. Another advantage of an opinion close is that it cuts straight to the point. You're directly asking the customer, "Is this working for you?" If the answer is yes, why isn't he buying? If it's no, then what is it that is stopping him from buying? If you're at a point with the customer where you feel comfortable asking for their opinion and they feel comfortable enough to be honest with you, then the opinion close is the right approach.

ASSUMPTIVE CLOSE

This type of close requires a great deal of confidence and some of the old "good vibrations" that the Beach Boys famously sang about. In an assumptive close, you don't ask or suggest. You assume. You assume that the customer wants to buy. You assume that you did your job well. You assume that the customer is convinced enough that it's time to go for the close.

Suppose you walked a customer through the demonstration, took her on a test drive and she is now sitting snugly in your office. You know, or are at least quite confident, that she wants to buy. Or, perhaps you simply want to try out your luck. Whatever the reason may be, you immediately choose to go in for the close but asking her to sign on the dotted line. Or, you say something like, "How would you like to pay?" or "Let's move on to your loan application."

In an assumptive close, a great deal depends upon your and the customer's frame of mind. For example, if you are feeling particularly positive and confident one day, you can employ the assumptive close artfully. On other days, it might feel a bit heavy handed or forced. If you have established a trusting relationship with a customer and he feels confident enough in your services, the assumptive close might work as well. However, you must not employ the assumptive close as your go-to closing technique, and you certainly must not use it on customers who were unwilling to buy in the first place. These customers might feel as though they are being forced and may end up not buying at all.

NOW-OR-NEVER CLOSE

This is another technique whereby you build pressure on the customer to purchase. Time is the main factor here—it's now or never; it's short notice; it's no-delay. You make an offer to the customer but intentionally limit it on the basis of time. They must buy now, not later. Not tomorrow. Not next week. You might tell them it's the last day of the limited-time offer. Or, if they sign today, they can get an extra 2% discount. Or, if they don't sign today, the product will be sold out tomorrow. "Now" is the important word.

Again, like the assumptive close, you must maintain a steady balance between subtly turning up the heat on the customer while making sure he doesn't feel that his is being pressured or forced in any way. And, just as with the other closing techniques, you must be aware of not just the nature of the customer but also his frame of mind at that particular moment in time. Can a limited-time offer compel him to sign more quickly? Can the sale or discount lure him in to close the deal? These are the questions to which you must know the answer before attempting this technique.

BALANCE-SHEET CLOSE

This type of close works best with analytical customers. Do you remember the analytical customers we discussed in the previous chapter? In order to convince this customer, you need to think and act like him. If he is analytical, you need to present an analysis. Learn from Benjamin Franklin. "My way is to divide half a sheet of paper by a line into two columns," he said, "writing over the one Pro and over the other Con." Grab a piece of paper and a pen, sit down with the customer and start channeling your inner Ben Franklin by making a list.

When using this approach, you need to consider your goal. Why are you employing this particular approach? You need to convince your customer to buy. Therefore, make the list as a salesman, not as a technical expert. The customer doesn't need a specialist's review of the vehicle. Your job is to assist him in making the decision, not complicate matters further. When you make a list, therefore, be sure to create a detailed pros column and a short cons column. Also remember to list the pros and cons out loud while you are writing them down. No one wants to sit in silence watching you write! A combination of audio and visual cues helps to stimulate the customer's thought process in a better way.

SUMMARY CLOSE

The Summary Close is somewhat similar to the balance sheet close and works well for the analytical customer. The main differences are: you don't write anything down, and you don't mention any disadvantages of buying the product. The formula is simple: present a comprehensive summary of all of the product's qualities, and move in for the close. Remember to make the vehicle sound as enticing as possible. This is the "selling" part. You are not only presenting a summary of the vehicle's features, you're selling it to the customer one last time before sealing the deal. Therefore, the content and presentation of the information you give are crucial. Remember to keep it detailed but not excessively so; you don't want to bore the customer.

The Summary Close is a great technique to use with the customer who already seems impressed by the product you have offered him. By iterating the product's best features one more time, you're hammering in the message that "this is a good product that fits your needs, and you want this. You really, really want this." You're creating an image in the customer's mind. You're using their imagination to show him how good your product is. You're helping him overcoming his instinctive hesitation to buy the product by stoking his inner thought process. There is virtually no harm in using this technique. It is also simply a much better alternative to directly asking for the close in most cases.

APOLOGY CLOSE

If all else fails, try an apology. Put simply, it works! Unlike other techniques, when employing this technique you won't put the pressure of decision-making on the customer. You will, instead, take the blame yourself. The script goes like this: "I'm sorry; I owe you an apology. I must have skipped over some crucial information somewhere along the way, and I'm sorry I couldn't be a better salesperson." You wouldn't believe how well this works in certain situations because it surprises the customers. Any conflict of interest you might have had is now gone. This approach softens the customer's stance, and might end up saying, "It's okay. It's not your fault. We just had a problem with the price."

You can now knowledgably move forward. Once they mention the price, you can restart the discussion with a focus on price. You can say, "I'm sorry I couldn't properly demonstrate to you that this is the best possible price you can get for this vehicle." The customer might say, "It's not your fault. We understand that this vehicle is perfect for our needs and modestly priced as well. It will just be hard for us to accept it at this price." Do you see what just happened? The customers agreed with you on the price. In one swift motion, you brought the customer exactly where you wanted him to be. Sometimes it's best to simply back off a bit and let the customers come to you rather than run after them.

---

7 Critical Rules of Closing a Deal

BELIEVE THAT YOU'LL CLOSE THE DEAL

If you skeptically begin pre-qualifying someone early on, you're setting yourself up for failure. You must believe that you can qualify *everyone* who comes into the dealership.

Don't take short cuts in order to attempt to qualify a customer. As long as you conduct a needs assessment shortly after your introduction, greeting and initial rapport building, you'll be able to determine what sort of vehicle to guide the customer toward to ensure that you can qualify them. It's your job to guide him to the vehicle that can best suit his needs, wants *and budget*. Don't take a customer on a test drive with a Land Rover if there is no way he can afford it.

At the same time, don't make a worth assessment based on the car the customer drives to the dealership or the watch he is wearing. People who have disposable income often appear as though they don't have it; people without it do what's necessary to make it appear as though they do. Treat them all the same.

SHAKE EVERYONE'S HAND WITH A SMILE

Believe me, you need to be shaking everybody's hand. Smiling is contagious, so be friendly. You will come across as the genuine person that you are. Shake hands with everyone in a party, including a customer's kids.

DRIVING SALES | 95

MAKE SURE YOU AND THE CLIENT ARE SEATED

When you are ready to begin discussing closing details, ensure that the client is sitting down—not walking through the parking lot, not standing next to a car in the showroom. Offer him and his party something to drink, and make sure they are comfortable. If they aren't sitting down, they'll be inclined to hurry and won't be as open to the deal you are proposing. If they're sitting, they'll be relaxed, and you'll have a better opportunity to close them.

TALK ABOUT EVERYTHING BUT THE DEAL

Once you're seated, it's important to quickly establish common ground. Therefore, don't start talking directly about the deal. Talk with the customer about where he's from (information you can easily gather from his application), and work to build genuine rapport—not simply be a hard closer.

Inquire as to how the customer chose to visit your dealership. It's imperative that you continue to build rapport with the customer even though the sales portion of the transaction appears to be over. Once the customer feels comfortable (tasteful jokes quickly go a long way toward making a customer comfortable), you can begin going over numbers.

CONFIRM THE TEST DRIVE

The biggest mistake salespeople make is talking numbers before taking the customer on a test drive. Most often, this happens because they've been burned by previous customers and, therefore, want to cut to the chase and see if a new customer will simply buy.

Be sure to ask the customer if he's had the opportunity to take his desired vehicle on a test drive. If not, stop the whole conversation and get him on that drive to make sure the car's options actually meet his needs. This step builds increased rapport and credibility as well as an emotional connection to a particular vehicle. If you skip this step, the customer can easily get to the close only to realize that the car doesn't have keyless entry or satellite radio, which is a deal breaker. Suddenly, you have to start all over (assuming the customer has time). While it may appear a shortcut, skipping the test drive is, more often than not, actually a time killer. The combination of speed, efficiency and a good transition is how you provide phenomenal customer service.

GO OVER THE WRITE UP

It's important to clarify, "This is the price we discussed, this is what your trade is worth, this is what the payoff is, etc." Break down every line item, and show the customer what his out-the-door cost is. Sometimes, explaining the terms and numbers in the paperwork will confuse the customer because he didn't hear part of it properly. If that happens, he may return the car or feel as though he didn't get a good deal, at which point he won't come back or recommend dealership.

ASK FOR THE SALE

I simply don't understand why people are afraid to ask for the sale. My approach is to go over the paperwork and then say, "Perfect. All we need you to do is sign and date right here." When you instead ask, "Well, what do you think?" the customer actually thinks about what he thinks!

Enthusiastically say, "Congrats! Here's your vehicle; all I need you to do is sign and date right here." Make it seem as simple as it actually is. The assumptive close is the simplest close you can attempt.

---

10 Common Closing Mistakes

Now that you know how to close the sale, it is essential to know how not to close the sale. Sales mistakes are the leading cause of frustration among many salespeople who are skilled, talented and employing all the useful sales techniques. Why, then, can they not close as many sales as their more successful counterparts? Even if you use all the techniques and tricks in the book and have the required skills to successfully close the deal, it may not work if you commit any of the following closing mistakes.

CLOSING TOO SOON

Two of the biggest sales mistakes that anyone can commit are closing ahead of or beyond the perfect time. If it were up to me to decide which is the bigger mistake, I'd say the former. Do not, I repeat, *do not* attempt to close too soon. When you do that, two things happen. First, you seem like a pushy salesperson. No one likes that. Second, you miss an opportunity to build trust with the customer. The trust gap widens because the customer thinks you're up to something. Remember Newton's third law: every action has an equal and opposite reaction. The harder you push, the more they will push back. Let me explain through an example.

Imagine yourself in the customer's shoes. Imagine that a sales representative were at your door, attempting to sell you a product that you were, curiously enough, interested in. You wanted to hear more about the product so that you could make up your mind. But the salesperson wasn't keen on convincing you about the product. He was only interested in closing. How would you feel? Would you buy the product? I certainly would not. I would think something "fishy" was going on. I would think there was something wrong with the product, even though it was probably fine. Closing too soon is one of the worst sales mistakes you can commit.

CLOSING TOO LATE

This is the other of the two closing mistakes—closing too late. This usually happens when the salesperson is too hesitant to ask for the close. If you are an experienced salesperson, you won't face this problem, since you will know exactly when you should close. But some of the newer salespeople I encounter commit this mistake often. What happens is, they reach the natural point in the conversation where it's time to ask for the close. But they don't do that. They continue on discussing the product. If you do that, you can easily provide the customers reasons not to buy the product or confuse them by droning on and on about details.

CLOSING WITH THE WRONG PERSON

We discussed the role of the influencers in the earlier chapter. If you didn't read the chapter and skipped right to this one, please go back and read it because it has lots of useful information. If you did read it—but forgot about the influencers—you are committing the same mistakes as the salespeople who try to close with the wrong person. To state the earlier information in a different way, in every sale with more than one customer, there is a primary person conducting the dealings and making all the decisions. That person is the key decision-maker. But the other people who accompany the decision-maker aren't exactly inconsequential. They are important. They are the influencers. Often times, salespeople try to close with the wrong person. They try to influence the decision-maker when they should instead influence the influencer. If a certain aspect of the product or the deal doesn't attract the decision-maker, it may attract the influencer. Don't waste precious time and energy with the wrong person. Many experienced salespeople admit to having committed this mistake in their earlier days. Almost every one of them was surprised to notice the impact on monthly sales of not focusing on the influencer.

FAILING TO NOTICE THE CLOSE

One of the most frustrating situations witness, as a sales manager, is seeing your team members fail to notice the close. I cannot tell you how many salespeople I have seen who continue to sell even after the customer is convinced.

They don't even realize that he customer is ready to purchase; he wants to give you his money. Are you willing to take it? Of course you are. So why not just ask the customer to close the deal? It saves you and the customer time while earning you a sale. It's a win-win. Don't let an opportunity like that escape.

DEPENDING DEARLY ON THE DEMONSTRATION

There's a misguided view that somehow crept into sales, perhaps when I wasn't looking. According to that view, if you demonstrate well enough, you've earned a customer. You don't need to close. The customer is already sold on the product. This is an absolutely false perception, if you think that the demonstration is the only thing that counts, you couldn't be further from the truth. Of course the quality of the presentation matters. It's also true that, without it, there is no sale. But those who depend on the demonstration to close the deal for them will fail to close as many deals as they would like.

This is why many car dealerships have "closers." These are experienced sales individuals who know how to close a deal. The only reason you need to bring in a closer is that the salesperson is not experienced or skilled enough to guarantee closing a deal. This shows how significant the actual closing is. A demonstration can only bring the customer so far. When you close, you're helping him cross the final barrier that stops him from buying the product.

NO RELATIONSHIP WITH THE CUSTOMER

Let's make this simple. If you want to sell 1000 cars per month, you need to start building a relationship with your customers. There is no alternative, no shortcut. How does this apply to closing the sale? While closing, your focus should not be on the sale itself. It should be on the customer. Don't think simply about how you can sell the car. Think how many times you can sell a car to the same customer. Think how many cars you can sell to the people who this one customer sends in. I'm telling you— it's a lot of cars. Before you know it, you could be selling 10, 20, or 30 cars a month on your own.

You must learn to employ addition to tact and wit, while selling. Emotional intelligence leads to the formation of long-term relationships with the customer. Were it not for emotional intelligence, salespeople would be extinct in the digital age. People would simply buy everything online.

But salespeople still exist, and we're important. And one of the things we can do better than a website is build an emotional connection with the people—make them laugh, capture their attention, and surprise and amaze them.

NOT UNDERSTANDING WHAT THE CUSTOMER WANTS

Another aspect of building a relationship with the customer goes all the way back to the first salesmanship skill we discussed: understanding what the customer wants. Without this understanding, you're not a good salesperson. Without it, you're not a closer. A lot of sales deals fail to close because the salespeople pitched what they wanted to sell, not what the customer wanted to buy. This is rookie mistake number one. This is why understanding the customer is so important. Make it a habit of asking the customer what they want early on in the process. Once you have that information, use it while demonstrating and, more importantly, use it while closing.

For instance, if safety features are what the customers are looking for in a vehicle, sell the vehicle that offers great safety features. Don't try to sell the vehicle you were assigned to push unless it best suits their needs. While demonstrating, speak about the safety features of the vehicle at great length. When you sit down to close the deal, go through them once more. Hammer it in. This is what you ask for. It won't get any better than this. It's exactly what you need to close a deal. If you truly understand the customer, you won't ever commit the mistake that comes next.

ONE-SIZE-FITS-ALL DEMONSTRATION

Do you want to lose a sales deal even before it has begun? If not, stop making a single memorized presentation to every customer you encounter. Stop proceeding to the demonstration without understanding what the customer wants. Most importantly, stop the outflow of random information that the customer is, probably, not even interested in. As they say, "People don't care how much you know until they know how much you care." Understanding the customer's concerns, and then modifying the presentation to meet those concerns go hand-in-hand. You cannot have one without the other.

Of course it's helpful to rehearse the presentation if you are relatively inexperienced or a little jittery. I understand that. And I advise my team members to do so. But, rehearsing doesn't mean that you have to recite whatever you learned in front of the mirror. Remember, it's not a stage play. It's a two-way communication even when you're the only one who's speaking. Learn to customize your presentation all the time. It's been said that no two snowflakes are exactly the same. I say that no two demonstrations should be exactly the same. Just like human beings, they must have character all their own.

NEGATIVITY

Salespeople not only sell the product, they sell the dealership as well. They must convince the customers that what you propose is the best offer they can get at the best dealership in their area. There are two ways to go about this. You can describe what sets your dealership apart, and you can describe how other dealerships are inferior. If you want to increase sales, always go for the first option. Stay positive. No one likes negativity. The impression it leaves on the customer's mind is, well, negative. Avoid that as much as you can. Rather than communicating that XYZ dealership offers less than your dealership, mention how your dealership can offer more than other dealerships. More is good. Less is bad. Remember this, and stay away from negativity.

This also applies when offering discounts to customers, especially when you're trying to attempt the Now or Never close. There are two ways to do this. First, "If you don't buy this today, you won't get a 2% discount." Second, "If you buy this today, you'll get a 2% discount." Do you see the difference? Which one do you think customers will respond to better? Offer carrots, not sticks.

BEING AGGRESSIVE

While we are on the subject of the Now-or-Never close, one of the worst things you can do is be too aggressive. If you try to pressure or bully the customer, even if he buys your product, he most certainly won't visit again. This is not the way to gain more customers. This is not the way to sell 1000 cars. In fact, it is counterproductive. Even if you are, through some miracle, selling 1000 cars per month by being aggressive, sales will eventually drop to 800, then 700, then 600 and on and on. It is a one-step-forward-three-steps-back approach.

Let customers breathe. Give them chance to ask questions. Allow them the opportunity to raise objections. Be patient. Address those questions. Remove those objections. Let them discuss their needs, and then work your way to meet them. Let them buy the product when they want. A little pressure is good, but forcing them to buy on your timeline is not. Being aggressive gives the impression that it's all about numbers and money.

This is how a typical sales process goes: you start by listening, and then move on to speaking, based on what you've heard. You then listen again, and speak again. It's a constant back and forth. Pushing your own agenda is the worst thing you can do in sales; avoid it at all costs.

The Follow-Up

A good follow-up is the difference between life and death in sales. It is how you transform prospects into clients and one-time customers into long-time customers. Following up with customers becomes all the more necessary when you consider our goal of selling 1000 cars per month. Most dealerships don't even receive 1000 walk-in customers in a month, let alone make 1000 sales. How, then, can you prepare your business to better achieve the goal. The answer is: a good follow-up.

Most businesses don't realize this. They either ignore the follow-up entirely or do not put great effort into it. The result? Best-case scenario: the level of sales stays the same. Worst-case scenario: sales go down, along with the business as a whole. This is why I have made follow-up the fourth and final stage of the sales process. Taking sales up to 1000 per month is simply impossible without good follow-up. No matter how good your marketing is, no matter how effective your salespeople are, no matter how affordable your prices are, no matter how brilliant your service is, good follow-up is a must.

4 Secrets to Mastering the Sales Follow-Up

In his book, *No B.S. Ruthless Management of People and Profits*, Dan S. Kennedy presents valuable approaches to significantly improving your follow-up game. Incorporating these five principles helped my team and me not only to close more sales from our leads but also to significantly reduce the time it took to make a sale.

First, it's important to note that there are three types of leads you work on during a marketing campaign:

Hot

Fresh out of the prospect oven, these are the leads you can sell to right away. This includes people who are already looking for cars. Saying the right thing can gain you a long-time customer. Just like other hot objects, you need to handle hot leads with absolute care.

Warm

This is where you focus most of your marketing attention. Why? In car sales, hot leads are a rarity. You cannot just find people who are looking for cars at any given time. Warm leads, on the other hand, are people who may buy a car in the near future. That "may" is the focus of your marketing strategy. You have to turn "may" into "will."

Cold

Cold leads are the customers who may never be ready. Many salespeople refer to these as bad leads or dead leads. You don't need to spend too much time on cold leads, but don't disregard them out of hand. A cold lead might turn warm one day. Therein, however, lies the crucial problem. While this list looks and sounds good in theory, in practice it is a different story altogether. How do you know which leads are which? A list of contacts doesn't offer much information apart from names and phone numbers. This is, therefore, where you and your team need to be proactive. You need to call each number to determine which kind of lead it is—hot, warm, or cold. Once you do that, reach for the low-hanging fruit first. But don't forget where the real money lies. Spend at least a bit of your energy on cold leads as well.

TIMING IS EVERYTHING

A perfect follow-up is only perfect because of the timing. This is the one factor that can make the difference between a random prospect and a sold customer. No matter how badly you want to sell, customers will only buy when they want to buy and when they're ready to buy. Timing is everything. To ensure perfect timing, you need three things:

Team

This one's a no-brainer. You cannot do everything yourself, and just as you need a dedicated team of salespeople to handle walk-in traffic, you also need a team that ensures effective follow-up.

System

Once you have a team of perfectly sales-people ready to their job, they need a system to follow. They need a method, and it's your job to come up with that. Stay tuned to find out how to create a perfect follow-up system.

Tools

With a team and a system in place, you're ready to set out on your follow-up journey. But wait a minute; aren't we missing something? Yes, we are; we are missing the tools the team needs to implement the system. Follow-up tools can range anywhere from a simple phone to complex software.

INTEGRATE SALES AND MARKETING

Integrating sales and marketing efforts works best for companies that conduct the bulk of their sales over the phone. Our business is a little different; we cannot sell a car over the phone. We usually need the customer to be physically present while we demonstrate the vehicle and close the deal. Does that fact therefore make this suggestion useless for our purposes? Certainly not.

Let's try to work our way around this complication by seeing how we, in the automobile trade, can integrate sales and marketing to produce the best results.

If your dealership has a marketing department and a sales team on the floor, do they function in collaboration? If not, they must. Since the salespeople are the ones who deeply understand the customers, they must be the ones to follow up with them. Marketing must be responsible for bringing in the leads, and the sales team must work on those leads. Only through complete collaboration can the car sales machinery function smoothly.

HAVE A LIVING CUSTOMER DATABASE

A lot of dealerships don't realize that a fully functional customer database can be the most valuable tool for customer follow-up. Just having a database does not magically solve all your follow-up challenges, however. You must constantly update, tweak, customize and modify that database to suit your increasing and changing circumstances. The database must contain the information of all leads, new and old, hot or cold, interested or unconcerned. It must contain the information of all the existing customers to whom you've sold vehicles. It must even have the order and billing information for these customers.

Another important thing to consider is that all the data must not be piled one over the other in a haphazard manner. Jumbled data is as good as worthless. You need valuable information at your fingertips. You don't need to be sifting through junk at the last minute. Your focus should be on being able to easily pick out the leads, customer, or prospects with whom you need to get in touch. You can do that through color-coding, assigning a score or points to customers on the basis of certain set metrics.

I considered all this and more when I set out to design my own customer database, theautominer.com. My two key goals were simplifying the target marketing and increasing customer retention. I spent hours, days, months, even years with the IT team perfecting the database. It now allows me to (for starters):

- Perform a quick and timely search for the right customers
- Filter search results on the basis of client or date
- Print, send and export emails and messages
- Create customer lists
- Create work plans
- Schedule, track and make calls

EDUCATION, REPETITION AND VARIETY

A perfect follow-up approach must contain the following three elements:

Education

A follow-up that's designed simply to gain customers can do wonders for you, but it doesn't help the prospects in any significant way. Instead, you must follow up in a way that brings some value to the prospects or customer. A good follow-up must inform and educate them.

Repetition

It's human nature not to pay attention to what we're not really interested in. Therefore, if you need to grab someone's attention, you need to be repetitive. That's the basic principle that under-lies all kinds of marketing, isn't it? Repeat your message over and over again so that it gets wired into the customer's brain. Follow-ups work the same work. You need to follow up with the customer again and again. Be repetitive. Be relentless. Be hungry. The repetition must not be disorganized or chaotic. It should be timely. It should be targeted. For instance, if a customer is not willing to buy a car right now but "may look into it next year," you need to be there next year. Because if you aren't, you just lost a customer.

Variety

The follow-up must be varied. Use different kinds of media to your advantage. You have physical mail, email, phone, fax and social media—so many ways to reach potential customers. Use all these means to your advantage in creating an effective follow-up strategy.

Following up with customers and prospects

Simply put, the follow-up is a process of keeping in touch with customers and prospects. Based on this definition, follow-ups can be classified in two ways:

- Following up with sold customers
- Following up with unsold prospects

How you interact with either of the two can vary based on the circumstances, although the intent is the same. You are looking to earn another sale, whether to a previously sold customer or a new prospect. The way to go about it can differ. Here are some of the best ways to follow up with customers and prospects.

SOLD CUSTOMERS

Once you've sold the vehicle, your job is far from over. Rather, it can be said that your job has only just begun. As a salesperson, your responsibility is not merely to sell. You must sell again and again. To do that, you need good follow-up with the customer. You need to build a relationship based on trust. This is the philosophy behind following up with the customers. This is what you need to bear in mind. The practical steps simply form the path that takes you to the destination. You can choose whatever works best. The four-step customer follow-up plan, based on our own process, is as follows:

1. Call the customer immediately after the sale. Thank them for the business. Inquire about their experience. Let them know you haven't forgotten about them. Let them know you care. You can also send them a thank you card. Sometimes small gestures work better than tried-and-tested means.

2. Call the customer two weeks after the sale. Explain to them the customer sales index (CSI) of your dealership. Ask them how they would like to rate your services.

3. Call the customer a month after the sale. Ask them if they would like to refer your dealership to the people they know.

4. Keep in touch with the customer periodically. The best, most passive and non-intrusive way is to send them monthly newsletters. Other options include sending greeting cards or emails on special occasions, such as Christmas or birthdays. Make sure not to send customary greetings. Each greeting must be personalized in some way. For instance, "How's Jenna?" Let the customer know that the greeting was created exclusively for him. Keep reminding him, in some way, to visit your dealership whenever he needs a vehicle. Make sure customers don't forget you.

PROSPECTS

Following up with prospects is not the same as following up with customers. You must jump into the process with a completely different mindset. Sold customers have met you. They know you. They've spent time with you. They've bought a vehicle from you. Prospects, on the other hand, barely know you. The dynamic of your relationship with them is not the same as with the customers. Your responsibility is to compel prospects to walk in to the dealership. Your job is to introduce yourself and the dealership to the prospect in the best possible light.

How do you identify a prospect? Are prospects only the leads that the marketing department generates? We discussed classifying leads into hot, warm and cold. But there's another kind of prospecting that few pay attention to. One of the biggest mistake salespeople commit in the follow-up is to ignore the customers who are "just looking." Granted, they probably won't buy a vehicle right away, but these are the most valuable prospects you can follow up with. Do not ignore them. Remember that, if they walked into your dealership to look for vehicles, they must really want to buy one at some point in the near future. These customers are the best kinds of leads you can generate. Include them as a priority in your follow-up process.

Here are some of the steps you can take to ensure an efficient follow-up with the prospects.

1. As the prospects are leaving the dealership, ask them why they don't want to buy a vehicle just yet. Is it the price? Do they want to research first? Do they have a particular vehicle in mind? Remember to note down the reason and some personal details such as their name. Call them a few days later, and ask if they've made a decision. Remember to include those personal details in your conversation. It leaves a good impression on the customer. It also helps forge that personal connection on which your dealership depends. This works particularly well if the

prospects were researching for the best dealership. An effective follow-up can go a long way.

2. Send them a greeting card or email to thank them for stopping by. Include your business card and ask them to visit again.

3. If budget was the issue holding them back, call them in a few weeks or months to ask them if the vehicle is now in their price range, or request that they visit your dealership when they make up their minds and are ready to buy a vehicle. Periodic contact ensures that the customer doesn't forget your dealership when he wants actually buy. If you have a new discount offer, make sure to call and inform them about it.

4. Send them a newsletter each month.

5. Even if they buy elsewhere, do not drop your contact with them. Avoid making them feel guilty for buying elsewhere. Instead, politely ask them to buy from your dealership in the future. If the other salesperson forgets to or does not contact them, you'll be at an advantage. Who knows, maybe you'll be ultimately able to gain another dealership's customer.

6. Even if the prospect is not willing to buy, you can always ask them for referrals.

Whether you're following up with a customer or a prospect, remember that frequency is crucial. Be careful of how often you establish contact with a customer. You need to be repetitive while not being intrusive. If you contact them too often, chances are they'll become annoyed, and you don't want that. If you don't contact them often enough, they may forget about you or buy elsewhere. You don't want that either. Maintaining a healthy level of follow-up frequency is absolutely essential.

Tips for an Effective Follow-Up

If someone approached me and asked me about an underrated way to build your sales up to a 1000 cars per month, I would answer with two words: follow up. If you don't do this, you cannot even think about selling 1000 cars per month, let alone actually attempt it. But, over the last decade, as I've learned a thing or two about sales, I have come to realize that following up is not enough. So I'd like to add another word to my earlier two-word philosophy and change my answer to this: effective follow-up.

How exactly do you do that? Is there a shortcut, a one-stop solution to an effective follow-up? Not exactly. There are, however, certain ways of doing things to ensure you're on the right track. You might say that a follow-up is only effective as long as the customer is willing to buy. If not, no amount of sales wizardry will sell your product. But there's a lot of ground to cover between customers who want to buy and those who don't. There are a lot of people somewhere in between. And you cannot reach them properly unless you effectively follow up. To do that, you must focus on the following tips.

CHOOSE THE BEST MEDIUM

Have you ever stopped to consider which medium is the best for a follow-up? Should you text or call? Should you leave a voice-mail or send an email? There is no single answer that is correct in every situation. There is no one "right" medium. Each is best for its own purposes. Each fits its time and place. It's up to you to choose the best medium for your purposes.

Email is the perfect tool for one-way communication. For instance, if you plan on sending a monthly newsletter, email is the best way to go. On the other hand, don't go near email if you are hoping to actually get a response from the customer. Some salespeople commit this mistake often. They prefer to email all prospects or customers since it's easy. It doesn't take much to type up a generic message and send it to a list of email addresses. But where's the fun in that? Where's the sales spirit? Where's the hard work? The customers feel that, also. Email removes the human element from the conversation.

Besides, even if the customer is willing to buy, email would unnecessarily stretch the conversation and make miscommunication more probable. There's an easy way to avoid that. Pick up the phone and call. Walk that extra mile. Do that and you'll clearly understand the difference. The customer will feel the difference. The beauty of sales will shine.

Another effective tool is social media. Unfortunately, it has been long-ignored by the car sales industry. It may take some time for my peers to realize this. But it is a fact that social media has completely transformed how sales are conducted. It's a way to reach a large number of people with just one click. And, more importantly, it's a way to receive valuable feedback. Make social media marketing an integral part of your sales strategy. Trust me, you won't regret it.

CUSTOMIZE YOUR MESSAGE

Have you ever found yourself on the receiving end of a sales campaign? I have. And there's nothing more pleasant than to realize that the salespeople remember you from a visit a year back. There's nothing more reassuring than realizing that the salespeople actually care. They consider you a human being rather than a walking pile of sales numbers, targets to be achieved to get ahead in the sales race. That feeling is beautiful. It's a breath of fresh air. And not just for me; many customers also feel that way.

You can try it yourself. Pick up the phone and make the customers feel that you care about them. You won't believe how many people you leave pleasantly surprised. Everyone expects salespeople to be sleazy. If you care about them, you can catch them off-guard. A gesture of humanity never goes unappreciated. The customers won't buy your product from a call, but they'll remember you. They'll remember you simply because you remembered them.

This is why you should avoid sending generic messages. Avoid it like the plague. Although the points you need to touch upon may be similar, always mold the message according to the kind of customer and the nature of the circumstances you're dealing with. Incorporate the customer's personal details in the message. Inquire about their health and wellbeing. Wish them well on special occasions. Off-hand comments customers make are critical, so write them down. Build on every personal detail you have. If you do that, you'll be able to build a personal connection with the customer. This will not only make customers happy, it will significantly increase the prospect of the sale as well.

AVOID "TOUCHING BASE"

Speaking of generic messages, what's more generic than opening the message with, "Hey, I'm just calling to touch base" or "Hey, just checking in"? Was there ever an opening so bland, an invitation so uninviting? If you want to achieve success in follow-ups, drop the term "touching base" from your vocabulary altogether. Imagine it doesn't exist. Imagine you need to find creative ways to open a conversation. Then do it, and wait for the sweet results. The way in which you open a conversation is important. Don't shut doors even before opening them by using such phrases as "just touching base."

Rather than something hackneyed or banal like, "I'm calling to follow up," why not be a little more creative while opening the conversation? Begin by asking the customer about his day. Impress the customer by recalling something he said in your last conversation. Open with a little pizzazz. For instance, rather than saying you're just calling to check up, you can say something like, "You mentioned in our last conversation that you were looking for vehicles with the best safety features. I'm calling to tell you that we have just the offer for you."

FOLLOW UP FOR A SPECIFIC REASON

Another reason to avoid "touching base" is that, if you take that approach, it communicates that you have no other reason to call than to determine whether or not the prospect is ready to buy. Granted, that's what it's all about, but the customer must not feel that. The customer must know the exact reason why you're calling, and it must not be the overarching sales purpose of "just following up;" the reason for your call must be specific. If you don't have one, find one. In my experience, customers always respond better when you have something to talk about. Having a well-defined agenda can remove the awkwardness of sales conversations.

On the other hand, following up for a specific reason relieves the customer of the pressure to say yes or no to the offer. It directs the conversation in another direction. This is called indirect selling—selling without directly asking the customer to buy—and it is the best option in these situations. Also, it gives the impression that you actually care about the customer's concerns. You're not selling the product just for the sake of numbers. You're selling the product because you want the customer to benefit from it. You're selling it to provide value to the customer.

For instance, consider this situation. You call a customer to "follow up" regarding whether or not they're ready to buy. The customer says no, and the call is over. Now, if you called the customer to discuss the specifics of a car deal, then you could've had a great conversation even if the customer wasn't willing to buy at that particular moment. You would have had a conversation nonetheless. You understand the wants of the customer better than ever now and, perhaps, the customer will remember you the next time you call. That's the difference between touching base and having a specific reason to call.

DETERMINE THE NEXT STEP

Never hang up the phone without having a concrete idea about the next step in the follow-up process. It could be anything—the next call, the next meeting, the next conversation, or the decision to buy. Don't let the customer go until you have an answer, until you receive some form of feedback. If you don't, you lose the whole purpose of following up. You don't want it to be an exercise in futility. You want a concrete outcome. Don't hang up before you have that.

How do we determine the next step? What exactly is it? The next step could be any of the options mentioned earlier. How would you know which option is the best? It's simple. You ask the customer what he wants. Ask him if it would be okay if you call again. Ask him what would the best way and the best time to keep in touch. Asking customers their opinions and keeping them involved in the follow-up process is essential. It establishes trust between you and the customer. It separates you from peskier salespeople. It moves the conversation forward on the customer's terms, not yours. Always attempt to build rapport with the customer instead of being intrusive or annoying.

In the best-case scenario, the customer may agree to buy the vehicle. In the worst-case scenario, the customer may ask you to stop calling. But, between these scenarios, there's an ocean of possibilities. It's up to you to know how to navigate through that. Some salespeople end the conversation with something vague like, "We'll be in touch soon." Don't do that. Instead, ask permission to call them on Thursday afternoon at 4:00, or two weeks later, or six months later. Whatever the timeframe, it should be specific. For instance, you're in conversation with the customer who's not interested in buying now but may be interested some time later. There's your opportunity. Ask, "Jim, can I call you in four months to see where you stand?"

MAINTAIN COPIOUS NOTES

If you and customer agree on a specific time to continue the follow-up, don't forget to write it down. Maintain notes. Maintain a lot of notes. These notes form your arsenal. Without them, there's no effective follow-up (unless, of course, you are some kind of a wizard who can remember trivial details about hundreds of customers, which you're probably not).

What would you actually take notes about? Notes may range from anything you remember the customer saying in your earlier conversations to the time of the next planned conversation.

For instance, if the customer mentions during the conversation that he was looking for a vehicle that offers him the most mileage at the least price, write it down. The customer mentions his price range. Write it down. The customer says that he's late and needs to pick up his children from school. Write that down as well. No matter how trivial the information may seem at the time, make a note of it. These precious little tidbits will help you enormously as you customize your email, time your next follow-up or have something creative to say while opening your next conversation. Remember I mentioned creating a follow-up system? This is the first step in that direction.

MAINTAIN A SCHEDULE

The second step in creating a follow-up system is to make a schedule of the follow-ups you need to conduct in the future. Create calendar entries for every customer. Don't be overwhelmed by an empty calendar. As soon as you make a sale, create an entry for the next day, two weeks later, and the following month. That way, you will create steady stream of entries. Afterward, note the appointments for the next follow-ups you will make with existing prospects, and enter those into the calendar as well. Take the leads that your marketing department managed to curate, and space them out on the calendar at regular intervals. Then, take another look at the calendar. It's not so empty anymore, is it?

Maintaining a schedule de-clutters all of your follow-up appointments and keeps you organized. In addition to that, it helps you to perfectly time your follow-ups. If you and the customer decided that you would speak next Thursday at 4:00, you'll be there next Thursday at exactly 4:00. It conveys a degree of professionalism that you cannot maintain without having a calendar. When everything's organized, you won't end up pulling out your hair in frustration. You'll know what to do and when to do it.

BUILD A FOLLOW-UP CUSTOMER DATABASE

Your notes and your schedule go hand-in-hand and collectively make up your customer data set. But it would be next to useless if there were no mechanism by which you could easily access it. That's why you need a customer database. This is the third and final step in creating a follow-up system; a functional database can be your greatest asset in the follow-up process. Make sure to update it regularly. Sit back. Relax. And let it do all the organization for you. A customer database can act as your personal assistant. Imagine coming to the office in the morning and having an assistant inform you about the meetings you have. That's the working principle behind a database. Each customer gets his own profile. You can access it to view the contact information, customer notes, next appointments, and the customer rating based on whichever parameters you've set.

These were the reasons that motivated me to create The Autominer, my own data-mining tool. Before it, follow-ups were a big hassle. I had so many details to note, so many appointments, and so many records of sales. I had bills, ledgers, and address books. The most difficult aspect of creating the database was going through thousands of files in order to recover all that information. I spent half my day sifting through piles and piles of papers. Not anymore. Everything is in a single place now. All I need to do is click on the customer's name and I can see everything, save valuable time, and spend all that newly freed-up time on the actual follow-up.

PICK THE PERFECT TIME TO CALL

The one thing that distinguishes an effective follow-up from a catastrophic failure is timing. This is what can make or break a deal. You need to decide the perfect time to make the call. How do you that? Is there ever a perfect time? What may be perfect for you may not suit the client and vice versa. It goes without saying that whatever suits the client is the right time to call. That's the bottom line.

How do you know what time works best for the customer? It's simple. You simply ask. Remember to note down the specifics, not the vagaries. Next week is vague. Next Thursday at 4:00 is specific. When it comes to choosing the right time to call, the client is king.

What should you do if this is your first call to the client and you don't know their wishes? Don't worry; I won't leave you hanging. I have a few tips of my own. If you noticed, I've been using Thursday in all my follow-up examples. There's a reason for that. Statistics show that Thursdays are the best time to call customers for follow-up. Not Tuesday. Not

Friday. Thursday. Data shows that Tuesday and Friday are the worst days to call. There's also evidence that Sunday and holidays may work as well, although I personally avoid those days.

Now that you know which days work best, is there a specific timeframe that usually yields the best results? Again, I have been using 4:00 pm in the examples because research shows that 4:00-6:00 pm is the best time to call, as the customer is expected to be more relaxed in the post-business hours. The worst time to call is between 12:00-2:00pm. It's imperative to mention here that these are the days and times that generally work best in sales. The most important thing is what the customer wants. If the customer wants you to call on Tuesday at 1:00, then that's what you do!

BE REPETITIVE BUT NOT PESKY

There is a huge difference between repetitive and pesky. Allow me to break it down. There are two components of this rule: how to be repetitive and how not to be pesky. Can we maintain a balance between the two? Sure we can. Let's examine the first one, and think about the proper ways to be repetitive. (There is such a thing and it is a fine line to walk). I've seen a surprising number of salespeople who give up after the first call. If you're one of those people, you can either pack your bags or vow to break that habit.

Calling once is not enough. In order for a follow-up to be effective, you need to call not once, not twice, not even thrice, but at least six times. Yes, you read that correctly—six times. This is not just a wild estimate; it's backed by statistical data. And the data is surprising. According to some surveys, a staggering 93 percent of converted leads are reached on the sixth attempt. Think about that for a moment. How many leads have you called six times? Not many, I bet. The reason so many sales are made on the sixth call is because most salespeople give up before that. The herd thins out, so you can reach the customer more effectively. They will listen to you because, by the sixth call, they have a pretty good idea about you, and you know exactly what they want.

Here's why a lot of salespeople fail at follow-ups: they think that if the customer didn't respond the first few times, the chances of them responding later are slim. This could not be further from the truth. In fact, more customers buy your product because you were persistent.

You took the extra step. You made one more call. You repeated your message so often that it left an imprint in their minds. So six (or more) calls it is.

How do you make those calls? Do you just pick up the phone and call them every day of the week? No. That would be counterproductive. You need to space out these calls on your calendar in such a way that the lead does not grow cold and you don't appear overbearing.

And therein lies our second component. Don't be pesky. This is tough when you have to call the customer six times. No customer, however eager to buy they may be, would want any salesperson to call them six times. You therefore must take that into consideration. There are several ways you can avoid appearing overbearing. The first is to provide value to the customer every time you call. If you are taking up their valuable time, make sure to give something to them in return. It could be anything—an article, a tip, some information, or a discount. Make the customer feel that spending time with you was worth it. You can also avoid appearing too clingy as a salesperson. Give the customers time to think about your offer, and don't sell all the time. Always prefer to have a conversation rather than a sales pitch. As Shark Tank investor Kevin O'Leary says, "Be sticky, not gummy."

INQUIRE ABOUT THE CUSTOMER'S CONCERNS

This is an important step to perform, particularly with sold customers. Remember, the demonstration was your job and earned you money and points when you closed the deal, but the follow-up is for the customer. Now that they've bought your product and spent considerable time using it, you can dig deep into the specifics of their buying experience. What did they like the most? What did they dislike the most? How was their experience in buying from you? What would they like to improve? These are all important questions that need to be asked but cannot be properly answered on the floor of the dealership. Naturally, the follow-up is the best time to do it. Let's examine these questions one at a time.

What did they like about the product? Asking about the problems when trying to receive customer feedback is obvious, but it's also essential to ask about the positives—what the customer liked about the product. This approach has many advantages. First, you get to know the customer more deeply. You get to know the kind of things he likes, so that the next time he visits, you can show him exactly what he wants. Second, and more importantly, when the customer states all the good things about the product, you are forcing him to look back and remember how wonderful his experience was. This is something he won't consciously do otherwise.

What did they dislike about the product? This is the most integral aspect of the feedback. When you know the customer's concerns, you'll be better placed to address them. Asking what they disliked is an interesting way to stimulate discussion. It not only gives the customer a chance to complain, it assures him that someone's listening, someone who cares, someone who can do something about his concerns. It can also enable you to report any flaws in the products to the manufacturers.

How was their experience buying from you? This is a really smart question because it's accomplishing two goals at the same time. On one hand, the customer can recall all that was good about your service and complain about all that was bad. On the other hand, it is a feedback mechanism. It's a mirror to show you how good your service really is. This is the only chance you'll have to get an evaluation of your performance through an outsider's perspective. It will present you with a set of problems for which you need to find a solution.

What would they like to improve? Again, this question is ingenious on many levels. Often times, I've been able to catch a customer off guard with this question. For instance, a customer raises an objection about, say, the way you demonstrated the vehicle, and you know the customer is wrong. You can't wait to show him how wrong he is. But you can't do that. So you wait. You patiently listen. Then you politely ask in what way they would like to improve the process. This is where they are typically left speechless and struggle to find an answer. Sometimes they will even accept that they don't have a better alternative. Finding problems is easy. Suggesting solutions is hard. Conversely, if a customer finds a genuine problem with your system and proposes an effective solution, even better. You're getting a free consultancy service while making the customer happy. Any salesperson would want to be in a situation like that.

When you ask about the concerns of the customers, you're also making sure that they know you care. You can assure them that if they come again or refer your services to their friends and family, they won't face the same problems. This way, you get the customers' commitment to getting you referrals while addressing their complaints. As I mentioned earlier, sales is a constantly evolving process. It evolves through trial and error as well as constant communication and solid feedback. The customers are the most important components of that process. The businesses that constantly transform their business models, that constantly innovate, and that actually listen to what their customers have to say are the businesses that succeed. Those that don't do any or all of the above are doomed to fail. It's time you decide which kind of business you want to run.

Driving Traffic

Whenever I entered the world of car sales, one of the most fascinating things I learned about the business was how to increase drive-in traffic. My Internet Director introduced me to some of the ways to increase walk-in traffic, and I instantly fell in love with the whole process. I was transfixed, enamored, and almost obsessed with finding ways to increase traffic. It was one of the reasons I achieved the level of success that I did as a salesperson. We had to grow as a dealership. We had to increase sales, and there could be no sales without customers. Failure was not an option. It was an uphill task.

I rose to the challenge. I held frequent, in-depth discussions with my boss about some of the ways to increase traffic. He would come to me with suggestions, and we had a constant back and forth. It felt like we were making scientific discoveries, searching for underlying laws that governed the universe of car sales. It was exhilarating, and I now want to share my exhilaration with you. I want to instill in you that sense of excitement, that aura of magic associated with this step.

THE IMPORTANCE OF DRIVING TRAFFIC

We came up with as many innovative ways to increase walk-in traffic as possible. The possibilities are endless, and

I'm sure there are differences between the ways various dealerships do it. Some believe in lowering prices, some don't. Some prefer TV marketing, while others utilize Internet advertising. There are a thousand different ways and no right way. In spite of all the strong differences, the disparities and contradictions, and the all-consuming competition and bitter rivalries, all businesses agree on one thing: driving traffic to the dealership is essential.

Without it, there are no sales, no goals, no techniques, no flashy showy campaigns, no revenue, no business. Without it, there's no way of selling 1000 cars per month. All the lessons in this book are meaningless if you don't drive traffic. All the skills, investments, and formulas will fail. All efforts to build a team are wasted. All meticulous planning to create a process is undone. Without those, you have nothing. You may as well close the dealership and find a new business.

If my views seem extreme, it means I'm on the right track. That's how much importance I attach to this step. This is the step without which there's no ladder. How can you sell 1000 cars per month if you don't even receive 1000 customers a month? You might have a brilliant team of salespeople, but they won't have anyone to demonstrate to. You might be situated on an ideal location but your rent will be a crushing liability without customers. You might be an effective sales manager, but you won't have enough money to pay your team's salaries. Your team will gradually shrink, and you will go backwards rather than forwards toward your goals.

20 Most Effective Ways to Increase Dealership Traffic

In my years of experience in car sales, I have tried nearly everything to increase traffic. I have constantly experimented. Admittedly, not all of the experiments succeeded. I fell face down, picked myself up, dusted myself off, and carried on. The experience was rewarding, to say the least. It was highly educational in terms of the dos and don'ts of driving traffic. At times, it was frustrating. We faced setbacks, hurdles, and failures. We went back to the drawing board again and again. We had to rethink our approach and come up with new and improved measures. And, if I may be honest, doing so was a tiring and taxing experience.

That's what I want to protect you from. You don't have to suffer setbacks like I did. Instead, you can build on the lessons we learned and the progress that we made. You need to push the boundaries further and further back. The automobile industry is advancing at lightning speed, and you need to keep up. These steps are, in no way, perfect. We're continuously improving, as should you. But you should not start from scratch. Do you honestly want to go through all the trouble that I described above?

Rather than doing so, consider these 20 ways to increase dealership traffic.

FAMILIARIZE YOURSELF WITH CURRENT TRENDS

Remember my advice about keeping up? (It was in the last paragraph, after all). Read it, absorb it internalize it. Keeping up is the first step of driving traffic. Familiarize yourself with the current trends in the automobile industry. You can find these trends in the newspapers, on the internet, in books, in seminars, and/or in other dealerships. More importantly, you find them in the study of your own sales. If you are observant enough, you'll find them everywhere. And observant you must be. If you want to be a good sales manager, if you want to increase traffic, you must be observant.

If you are observant, you likely will have noticed that buyer behavior is changing. The walk-in traffic has different expectations than it did "back in the day." Walk-in customers have different needs, different drivers, and different motivations. They are smarter and more cautious than before. If you need to increase traffic, you must understand buyer behavior. Not just globally or domestically—you need to understand what motivates your local buyers to walk into a specific dealership.

There are many ways to do that. Some of them are pretty obvious. Newspapers and the Internet can be valuable resources in assessing the general outlook of car buyers nowadays. But if you need specific data, you need to get your hands dirty. You need to go out in the field. Conduct local research and surveys if you must. Go to the buyer if the buyer doesn't come to you. Gather data and do an analysis. This must be the first step in any attempt to increase traffic. If you understand buyer behavior, you can shape the next steps to attract more customers.

BE UNIQUE

Driving traffic to the dealership is essential, but the way you go about it is even more critical. I have seen many dealerships invest all of their considerable energies into driving traffic through traditional means such as lead-generation and chasing customers through phone calls and appointments. This is a fundamentally flawed approach. Granted, these steps are necessary for driving traffic, and there can be no increase in sales without a focus on these steps. In addition, however, you must consider how much of your energy you devote to it. The top managements of such dealerships are often frustrated by the lack of results despite all the hard work that they put in pursuing customers.

But these dealerships are forgetting one simple—but important—fact. Customers don't come to you because you ask them to; they come to you when they see value in it. They come to you because of that one element that sets you apart from other dealerships, that one element that makes you unique. Therefore, if you want to increase the number of walk-in customers, ask yourself this very basic question: what sets us apart?

Customers are smart. I feel the need to repeat this point in order to bring it home. Customers are smart, and they are perceptive. They are shrewd and observant. When customers leave their homes and enter a dealership to buy a vehicle, they know exactly what they are doing. They compare and contrast all local dealerships. They do their research. Do you? If you don't, you should. An easy way to do this is to make lists of what all the other dealerships in the area, all your competitors, offer. Make lists of why customers may choose those dealerships over you. Once you have all the data, ask yourself what sets you apart. What can you offer that other dealerships cannot? What makes you better?

While answering these questions, don't include intangible or unquantifiable elements such as "quality of salesman-ship" or "trust and care." There's no way to measure these qualities. Always include quantifiable factors. What do you offer the customer that can be measured? Some of the answers may include special discounts and competitive prices.

DON'T LOWER YOUR PRICE

Speaking of prices, it is important to have a frank discussion about lowering prices to increase the number of walk-in customers. Why do you want to drive traffic to your dealership? To achieve your sales targets, right? Why do you want to achieve targets? To increase sales, right? Why do you want to increase sales? To generate more profit, obviously! It is the sole reason for which you're in business. Why, then, do you need to cut down on those very same profits in order to attract more customers? Doing so beats the entire purpose of the exercise; it makes no sense.

If, for instance, you cut down on your profits by 50 percent and receive 50 percent more customers, the net result is the same. It's only an illusion of movement. You think you're going up, but in reality all you did was take one step forward and two steps back. You're standing in the same position.

Another (more critical) aspect of lowering prices is, it's the one thing that every dealership can do. Anyone can lower prices. When you do it, others will do it as well. Before you know it, you're in a price war, which is uncharted territory. You don't want to go there. If you get into a price war, you need to lower your prices in order to thrive—to survive even. And in a price war, there can only be one winner. There can be only one dealership with the lowest prices. If price were what closing the deal came down to, most customers would choose the dealership with the lowest price from the start. If you're not that dealership, you just lost the price war and all the customers that came along with it.

The more sensible thing to do is to avoid the mess altogether. Keep your prices competitive, but don't lower them in order to attract customers. If you need to drive traffic to your dealership, look elsewhere to do so. This is where the next step comes in.

FOCUS ON VALUE-ADDED SERVICES

Instead of lowering prices, focus on providing more value to the customers in exchange for the money they pay you. Diversify your services. Provide unique offers. Focus on value-added services. This step has the essence of all of the earlier steps. It is what you should do instead of lowering prices. It is what will set you apart, and it is how you keep up with the trends. Let's analyze these three activities, one step at a time.

I mentioned that lowering prices is an action any dealership can take. However, not all dealerships can—or do—provide value-added services. This is why doing so is a healthier alternative to lowering prices, and it's what will set you apart from your competitors. When we analyze current trends, this is what we see happening everywhere. Dealerships are reducing prices and offering discounts, but they still cannot attract customers. This is why they are turning to value-added services. Hyundai has launched an online portal for car servicing. Toyota is focusing on offering easy financing to their customers so that they can buy their vehicles. BMW has created an in-house call center to reach out to new customers.

Do you notice the common thread in all of this? These brands are not selling cars by trying to, well, sell cars.

They're selling cars by other means; they're attracting their customers through other means. This is what good value-added services can do—more than price reductions, more than discounts. You need to focus on this rather than using traditional means to attract clients such as conventional advertising and hackneyed solutions. You need to provide unique warranties, maintenance packages and free car washes to customers. Not only does that set you apart from your competitors, it also drives the competition in a desirable direction. Trust me when I say this. Competing on services is far better than competing on prices.

CREATE SMART ADVERTISING CAMPAIGNS

I don't need to tell you the benefits of advertising. Advertising is integral to attracting more traffic to your dealership. I'm not here to stress on the importance of creating advertising campaigns. That's a given. What I do want to discuss instead is how to create more effective advertising campaigns, how to create, as I call it, smart advertising. If you have a strong business sense, you won't face many challenges with this step.

Imagine advertising as a business venture. It's a process of making business investments and then reaping returns on those investments. And, like any successful business, you need to minimize investments and maximize returns. How do you maximize returns on advertising, and what exactly are returns on advertising? A simple way to describe returns on the business is, it is the money that ends up in your pocket at the end of the day. Returns on advertising function in a similar manner. Instead of calculating money in your pocket, you calculate the number of customers brought into your dealership by end of day.

To create an effective advertising campaign, you must bring in the most customers at the lowest cost. That is the essence of a good investment: spend less to earn more. So get down to it. Create targeted advertising campaigns. Focus on the best mediums to spread your message. Spend your energy reaching the right people rather than simply reaching more people. Find innovative ways to advertise. Observe what your competitors are doing. Analyze the rights and wrongs of their strategies. Search for ways to top them. Identify your own strategy in order to beat theirs. Devise. Revise. Improve. I realize that this advice may seem vague. It is. I'm painting the picture with a broad stroke at this point. I'll get down to the specifics of the process one at a time, and in order to do so have dedicated the next few steps to the discussion of different aspects of advertising.

USE MULTIPLE MEDIUMS

The influence of technology is a recurring theme when finding ways to increase walk-in traffic. More and more dealerships are embracing that technology. More and more dealerships are leaving traditional means like newspapers, TV, and radio behind to fully embark on organized online advertising campaigns. That might be too extreme a course of action from the get-go. I would advise you to focus on both traditional and modern means simultaneously.

Create TV ads, radio ads, and online ads. If a message is repeated often enough, and through various different mediums, it has an increased chance of leaving an imprint on the audience's mind. For instance, if a customer switches on the TV and sees your ad, switches on the radio and hears your ad, and then goes online and clicks your ad, the message might sink in. Another advantage of a multiple-medium advertising campaign is that it conveys the message to wider audiences irrespective of age or background.

The most significant consideration while creating multiple-medium advertising campaigns is ensuring that you are targeting it to the right potential customers. There is no point in spending money on your advertising campaign if your ads aren't reaching the desired demographic. Crude numbers don't do anything beneficial. If an ad reached 100,000 people in general, and another ad reached only 100 people who are genuinely interested in your product, the latter is preferable. Numbers are not the most important aspect of an advertising campaign; what lies behind those numbers plays a significant role as well.

In TV and radio, you should focus on local channels rather than big networks. Narrow down the time of day at which you can reach the widest possible audience. Try to find relevant programs that cater to people who are interested in automobiles. Rather than blasting out your message to the most people, try to carefully convey the message to those who care.

POST ONLINE ADS

Targeted ad campaigns are also essential in online marketing. In fact, online ads let you target audiences far more effectively than traditional means such as TV or radio. You can find local audiences, use key search terms to narrow down prospects, and find specific websites associated with car sales in your area. There's so much to do, and such a wide range of options. If you do this right, if you play your cards well, you're sure to be successful.

The best way I've found to create targeted online ads is to make a list of the biggest automobile websites that people access to conduct pre-purchase research. Narrow down your audience by targeting prospects around the geographical area where your dealership is located. Tailor those ads to suit the audience's needs. Make them attractive and appealing. Then sit back, relax, and watch customers walk into your dealership in droves.

Research suggests that online advertising is the game-changer in the automobile sales industry. It is what's shaping the current trends. A 2014 report by the Interactive Advertising Bureau provides valuable insights. According to the report, people who are looking to buy a car are 71 percent more likely to be influenced by online advertising than other consumers. Almost 75 percent of car buyers are more likely to own smartphones, 66 percent regularly watch online video commercials, and 58 percent research online before buying a product. So, now that we have enough data to ascertain how essential digital marketing is, let's move on to how to do it.

One of the most significant means of online marketing is pay-per-click (PPC) advertising. Other means include banner or display ads, micro sites, and third-party advertising. There is no single means on which you must focus. A proactive online advertising campaign usually relies on a combination of all these means.

FOCUS ON A SOCIAL MEDIA STRATEGY

Even though a lot of dealerships are coming around to realize the importance of online ads, many are still unaware of the impact of another medium of online advertising: social media. It surprises me to see how many dealerships don't take social media seriously. Maybe they don't realize its impact. Maybe they think it is a medium that cannot be utilized for professional or commercial purposes. Maybe they don't know that social media is one of the most effective means for online advertising. Whatever the reason may be, they're missing out on a great opportunity.

Social media offers an array of options for brands to capitalize on marketing opportunities. So widespread is the influence of social media that marketing experts are forced to seriously analyze its impact and find ways to create an effective social media strategy. And this is exactly what your dealership needs—a social media strategy that generates results. Although the social media strategy must incorporate most of the popular social media platforms into your marketing process, the most effective platform is Facebook. This is where most of your attention should go. This is the platform that will generate the most walk-ins.

There are a number of ways to drive traffic through social media. Obviously, your dealership needs to have a Facebook page. Facebook provides the option of creating a customized landing page. This is where you will generate most of your leads. You can use this page to advertise new offers and promotions. For instance, if you're offering test drives on a particular vehicle, ask visitors to submit in their contact details, and you've got yourself a lead generator. These leads are hot off the stove. They're the highest quality leads, and the type that you won't find elsewhere. You can create paid advertisements through Facebook, organize Facebook contests to attract visitors, and post your activities on other pages related to the community you specifically wish to target.

CREATE AN INTERACTIVE WEBSITE

Like online advertising, most dealerships have come to realize the importance of creating a website. Almost all of the major dealerships have created a web presence, which is an encouraging sign. Whether they're doing it right, however, is another matter. The first step in creating a website is identifying the reason behind designing the website. If your purpose is to drive more walk-in traffic to your dealership, you should design the website in a way to be able to do that. A website can serve multiple purposes as long as they are each clearly outlined. Without doing so, you're shooting in the dark. You need to know what you need to do before you do it.

Whether you are creating a new website or re-designing your existing one, you need to understand some basic rules. A website must be designed in a way that a customer can complete the same activities as they would if they physically came into your dealership. It must be fully up-to-date with the entire inventory. In addition, every product must have a detailed description as well as links to reviews and other resources. If customers do their research on their website, they're more likely to trust and buy from your dealership.

Your website is also your marketing platform. It's the location where you can place as many ads as you like for free. It's your playground. Go crazy, but be creative with your promotions. No one wants boring ads that look make it look like the dealership is trying to sell them products. Be cool. Be innovative. Entertain and educate your customers. After all, they've visited your website, so they are your guests. Make sure they have a good time.

Perhaps the most important function of the website is lead generation and increasing walk-in traffic. For that, the website needs to be interactive. On every page, the customer must have a clear opportunity to get in touch with the dealership. It's important to obtain their email address and contact number. Once you have that, you have a customer.

Along with leads generated through social media, leads generated from the website are of the highest grade—perhaps even more so. Don't let these leads slip away from you at any cost.

DON'T FORGET SEO AND WEB DESIGN

There's is no point in creating a website if you don't expect to have visitors on it. And there's no point in expecting visitors if you don't do search engine optimization (SEO) because most traffic comes from search engines. Except your staff—and likely your most loyal customers—hardly anyone visits your website directly. They all come through search engines. If you want more visitors, you need SEO. It can be simply defined as the process through which you make your website more visible in the unpaid or "organic" search engine results.

Most experts consider SEO to be one of the most effective strategies for advertising online. You can do it in-house if you have the skills, know-how, and expertise. But it's always better to contact a professional. It won't cost much compared to paid advertisements, and the results will be long-lasting and reliable.

Dean Evans, the chief marketing officer for dealer.com, is so confident in the power of SEO that he considers the efforts that go into improving your website's search rankings "purely the best ROI you can get for any activity you can be doing at the store, period." What more is there to say?

Finally, there's the visual design of the website. According to research by Stanford University, nearly 46 percent of respondents consider a company's website design to be the most important factor in determining whether or not the company is credible. There are many general car dealership web templates available online. Don't use them. How can you ensure that your dealerships unique attributes can be represented accurately online if you attempt to fit everything into a pre-designed template? Not to mention the fact that countless other dealerships, some of them possibly being your competitors, are likely using the very same template. Another thing to consider while designing a website is the importance of making it mobile-friendly. As I mentioned, nearly 75 percent of potential automobile buyers own and use a smartphone. This is a huge demographic, and you cannot wish to create an efficient design without trying to incorporate them into the general picture.

GENERATE CONTENT

The last—and one of the most important—aspect of online marketing is generating content. Without it, you cannot create a website. Without it, you cannot sustain a social media presence. Without it, you cannot offer value to your customers online. But before we begin to examine how to generate content, we need to consider what exactly content is. How do we define content? What are its different types? When we say "content," we are referring to what is generally known as "web content." It can be either text-based, visual or both, and it is a huge part of the user experience on the website. The most relevant types of web content that can help you reach more customers include blogs, images, videos, infographics and promotional materials. These are the kinds of content on which you need to focus.

The foremost among these are blogs. Blogs are the best way to provide value to your customers, the best way to increase the shareability of your content and, by extension, your dealership's name. Research suggests that the brands that maintain a blog generate 67 percent more leads per month than those who don't. Let me restate the difference. 67 percent more leads per month. I'll let you calculate how many leads you generate per year and over longer periods of, say, five years. That's a lot of leads and, consequentially, a lot of walk-in customers.

You can also create videos since they are more visual media and preferred by some as an alternative to reading. The videos must be entertaining, educational and promotional.

Another content type is the monthly newsletter you send to your clients or subscribers. Web content also helps you create better follow-up emails that don't just "touch base" but are actually more informative and interactive for customers.

Another popular form of shareable content for dealerships includes stories of customers' good experiences with your dealership. This is a very smart content strategy since it does two things simultaneously. First, human stories or experiences are always relatable. Potential prospects now have actual proof that your dealerships provide better service than others. Second, these stories are a better way to conduct promotions without it looking like you're strictly trying to sell cars.

USE ATTRACTIVE PROMOTIONS

All of your smart advertising will fail miserably if you don't actually have something to offer to customers. Offering enticing promotional deals is, therefore, at the heart of all techniques to increase walk-in traffic. If you offer promotional deals that set you apart, and if you're able to advertise those offers effectively to the customers, you have a recipe for success. This is the one step that every dealership knows will bring in traffic, but few are actually successfully able to leverage these promotional offers to attract more customers. Let's analyze some of the promotional deals you can offer to drive more traffic to your dealership.

Sponsorships: Instead of creating boring promotional campaigns and advertisements, spend your marketing allowance to sponsor a local team. It's a good way to throw your dealership's name out there.

Express Saturdays: Since many customers are busy during the week, and the weekends are the busiest day of activity for many dealerships, you can make the most out of them. Through express Saturdays, you can offer discounts and special maintenance deals for customers who cannot make it to the dealership on weekdays.

Games: Who doesn't love games? You can create fun activities for your customers, and offer them a chance to win discounts and gifts. Who says marketing has to be boring? Maybe you can have some fun, too.

Customer rewards: Why should customers buy at your dealership? Why should they even set foot in there? Do they get anything in return? They can, if you create a program of rewards. These rewards can range from discounts and complementary purchase offers to movie tickets and dinners for test drives. Instead of rewarding only those who buy, you can even attract those customers who are "just looking." Good customer care is the key to creating long-term relationships.

USE THE CUSTOMER DATABASE

We come back to the database again and again because having a customer database is that important. We won't again discuss why you need a customer database. Instead, I want to explain how to use that database to generate more drive-in traffic. I regularly use my own customer database theautominer.com for this purpose. Your existing customers and leads are your biggest resource. It's with them that your biggest chances of generating traffic lie. Therefore, you should naturally rely on the customer database like I do. Let's examine some of the ways you can do that.

Two of the primary ways to generate more drive-in traffic are repeat clients and referrals. Your existing customers have had an experience with your dealership. You practically don't even need advertising to create repeat clients. You simply need a bit of effort in improving customer service. You need to form a human connection with the customers. If you provide good customer service and properly follow up with the customers, you not only improve your customer service rankings but you also significantly increase your floor traffic. Good service can also lead to good word-of-mouth, and that generates traffic through referrals—another important reason for more people to walk in.

My customer database, theautominer.com, not only helps me keep track of existing customers, it also helps me keep track of potential leads I've generated through social media, our website, and other means. It helps me keep track of my progress with these leads. By keeping extensive notes and lead information, I can ensure an effective follow-up process. This, in turn, generates more walk-ins to the dealership. What more could a sales guy want?

CONDUCT COMMUNITY SERVICE EVENTS
Is there a better way for local dealerships to reach out to their community than by participating in community service events? I don't think so. I always stress the importance of advertising without it appearing as though you're trying to

sell something. There is simply no better alternative for this than community service. Not only are you advertising your brand, you're actually doing good for the community. This is a great way to drive traffic to your dealership. Community service events bring in lots people who are from the community itself and may want to buy vehicles. Admittedly, not all of them will turn to you to buy a car. In fact, most won't. But you're not in business simply to sell cars. You're there to make a name for your brand in the community—a reliable name that people can trust and associate with good deeds.

You can also organize your own community events to familiarize more people with your dealership. If you are new to the business, there's no better way to capture people's attention. Moreover, you'll be able to bring more people to the sales floor. How many customers you are able to retain or bring back depends upon your skill and service.

Some of the community events that you can organize or participate in include hospitals and charity events. You can conduct blood drives, food drives, and toy drives. You can hold events related to vehicle safety awareness. Once you capture the attention of your audience, it's easy to introduce them to your dealership and inventory. You can decorate the event space with advertisements and promotional material. You can promote the events through social media or post ads in newspapers to get maximum attention. If you want to increase walk-in traffic, you need to be proactive.

TAKE THE VEHICLES TO THE PEOPLE

Are the people not coming to see how amazing your vehicles are? No problem. Take the vehicles to the people!

Your need to sell the vehicles is greater than people's desire to buy them. It is natural that you should take the extra step, walk the extra mile, and do something that none of your competitors is doing. Put your inventory out into the community. You can display your vehicles at community events and exhibitions. Sporting events and shopping malls are also a great place to display your vehicles.

Why make all that effort when you have a display in the dealership? The purpose here is to stimulate people visually. It's one thing to search for vehicles online or read reviews. It's another to see the brand new vehicle in all its glory. It instantly captures the customer's attention. And you have a salesperson ready to demonstrate the vehicle to the customer right there on the spot. You can also reach a wide number of people with a single demonstration. And, if the people learn about the vehicle from you, they're more likely to buy it from you as well.

This is also a great way to promote certain vehicles that you want to sell. It's a much more effective strategy than trying to push the vehicle to the customer who doesn't want to buy it. By putting your preferred vehicle in the spotlight, you create a demand for it among potential customers. This approach works great as a form of subliminal advertising. Even if people don't actively come to you for information on the vehicle, they register its appearance and will likely subconsciously prefer to buy that particular vehicle when they walk in to your dealership.

OFFER TEST DRIVE INCENTIVES

Winning over some people is hard. No matter how much you promote your vehicle, how attractive your promotions are, and how successful your advertising is, they won't budge.

That is, not until they actually sit in the vehicle and drive around the block. That's why test-drives appeal to so many people. After all, there's no harm in driving a vehicle for a bit. Afterward, the customer seems to like it, and he is actually interested. By simply offering a test drive, you can bring your customer to the table. It's amazing how such a simple measure can yield such effective results.

What you must realize is that, when you offer a test drive, you don't just offer a test drive. You offer the whole package. You urge a customer to win something else by doing a test drive. For instance, the customer can win tickets for his family to view the latest blockbuster movie just for completing a complimentary test drive. Or, drive with us and win free dinner at a local restaurant. These are both attractive deals because not only is the customer getting a free test drive, he has a chance to win something else by doing so. Who wouldn't want that?

Test drive offers are also a great way to promote your brand. You can organize social media campaigns around them. You can run ads on TV and in print. A particularly effective way to promote a test-drive deal is through emails and phone calls. When you offer a test drive to a potential prospect through one-on-one communication, it adds an element of exclusivity to the whole process. It may seem like a hassle to let so many people drive your vehicles without any guarantee that they'll bye. It can be inconvenient as well. But if you get one interested prospect out of 10 test drives, it's a success.

PARTNER WITH DRIVING SCHOOLS

We have discussed sponsoring local teams and participating in community events. It's time to move on to something that is more in line with the nature of our business. Participating with driving schools makes sense in many ways. First, who better to participate with a driving school than a car dealership? Not only are we qualified to do that, we understand the requirements of such a relationship. Second, and more importantly, if someone's learning to drive, there's a good chance that he, or someone he knows, will buy a vehicle in the near future. So it's a smart publicity tool as well.

Another thing you can do is to partner with local schools and colleges that offer driving education. Potential customers can be found anywhere. You just need to know where to look. Potential drivers can also be the best resource for potential customers. You can ask the driving instructors to recommend your dealership in the event that students want to buy a car. You can also offer promotional deals to the students. For example, a referral through the driving school provides the buyer with free maintenance or a complementary car wash. If you start off on the right foot with these new customers, you create the potential for a life-long relationship and countless referrals.

FOCUS ON CREATING REPEAT CLIENTS

I imagine that, if you have up until this point, I don't need to reiterate the importance of focusing on creating repeat clients. But I believe it is imperative to again mention the fact that repeat clients are essential to increased walk-in traffic. We discussed the importance of creating long-term relationships, and the fact that there are numerous benefits to doing so. It doesn't only improve customer satisfaction ratings, it also convinces your customers to buy fro you a second time, and a third, and so on. Create repeat clients who trust you and invest full faith in your abilities.

How can repeat clients lead to increased walk-in traffic? Let's start at the beginning. The average American owns six cars in his or her lifetime—per person, not for the family as a whole. A husband and wife, on average, own six cars each in their lifetimes. And then there are kids. If you treat your customers properly, and focus on building longer-term relationships, all these potential sales can be yours. Let's put that in perspective. Let's say you sell cars to 30 customers in a month. Assuming they're all happy, each of them will come back to you to buy again. If each of them buys 6 cars in a lifetime, you're looking to sell as many as 180 cars over your career, simply by focusing on thirty clients. Multiply that by 12 months in a year and by as many years as you'll stay in business. I don't need to tell you that that's a lot of cars!

Selling cars can be easy. Sustaining sales is not. Earning money by making a sale is undemanding. Continuing to earn from the same customer is not. This is why many dealerships fail and why not many are able to drive walk-in traffic onto the sales floor. Your repeat clients form your support base. The initial sales are merely the tip of the iceberg. Repeat business is what lies underneath. Sure, you can employ cheap tricks to artificially boost sales for a few months, maybe even a few years. But that's not an iceberg; that's just some ice piled on a raft. Sooner or later, the ice will melt or the raft will sink. And your business will sink with it.

ASK FOR REFERRALS

When you treat the customers well enough to earn repeat business, you will naturally get a lot of referrals as well. But it's not a given; there's no guarantee that your clients would refer your business to other clients. You have to work hard to ensure that they do. This is when we refer back to the customer database. It's a multi-purpose tool, and using it to ask for referrals is another one of its purposes. It's also one of the reasons to follow up with the sold customers. When you call them, you're basically reminding them to refer your business to other clients. And there's no harm in saying that upfront.

After repeat clients, asking for referrals is the second technique that relies on customer service. They go hand-in-hand. If you have repeat clients, you will have plenty of referrals. But repeat clients aren't the only source for referrals. Ask for referrals when you cold-call prospective leads. Do it while you're out in the field to promote your vehicles. Do it when you're dealing with the "just looking" crowd. Do it while participating in a community event or offering a sponsorship. Don't hesitate to just ask.

These referrals will be a huge source of walk-in traffic. It's essential to consider here that the nature of the walk-in traffic is different from the numbers of the people who step in to your dealership. Referrals, unlike some walk-in customers, don't just happen to stumble across your dealership. Someone sent them, someone whose opinion they trust. That's why it's easier to work with them. It's easier to convince them of your reliability since they already have a sense of it through contact with a sold customer. This is why referrals are a treasure. Aim to preserve what you have and gather more in order to get rich.

OFFER DISCOUNTS

Since offering discounts is the most obvious strategy to increase drive-in traffic, I've decided to include it at the end. Ideally, you know much more about discount pricing strategy at this point. Still, it doesn't hurt to say a few more words about it. I don't recommend lowering prices or getting involved in the downward spiral of a price war. But discount offers are okay—better actually. If you know to leverage discount offers in order to drive in more customers, and if you know how to properly market those offers, discounts can be beneficial for business. Let's examine some of the types of discounts you can offer and the impact these offers may have.

The first thing you need to consider the purpose of the discount. Whatever the purpose may be, the nature of the discount must be molded to fit the purpose. For instance, if a discount is created in order to stay competitive, you should go out and analyze what your competitors are offering, and then shape your offer accordingly. If you are including a discount in order to attract new customers, it must be enticing enough to appeal to new prospects. If you want to reward existing customers, you need to set a criterion on which to reward and determine how much to offer. All these considerations are important while shaping discount packages. You don't want to utilize a strategy originally designed to earn more profit only to find that it's costing you valuable money.

There are many types of discount offers, and which you select depends upon the reasons behind creating that offer, some of which are mentioned above. Some of the offers that work best include loyalty cards that offer special discounts to reward, well, loyalty. Another interesting and effective way to use discounts is to offer them as gifts or prizes for the games you organize in your dealerships, on social media, or in community events. This is a smart strategy since it not only attracts new customer, it also promotes your dealership in a way that's fun and engaging.

There are also seasonal discounts that are offered during peak sales times. It's useful to have one or another discount offer going at a given time since it gives you an excuse or a reason to market your product to wider audiences.

VELOCITY MANAGEMENT

When it came to driving traffic to our dealership, the Velocity Management program greatly helped me. What exactly is Velocity, and how does it work? The Velocity® program was developed by Dave Pollack, inventor of vAuto and author of various books on the subject. His velocity books greatly helped me to harness the proper tools and gain insight into the process of boosting my sales through driving more and more walk-in customers to the dealership. I recommend his Velocity® book series to all salespeople who are hoping to achieve similar results.

Although originally designed as a method of used-car management, the Velocity Management program can be as efficiently applied to automobile sales in general. The automobile industry has transformed rapidly over the past decade because of the Internet. Consumers are much smarter, profit margins are much lower, and competition is much fiercer. It's a cutthroat environment, and car dealerships have to adapt to survive. The Velocity Management program assists dealerships in doing that by increasing the volume of sales rather than trying to garner more profit on a specific vehicle. It relies on employing technological tools and better information in order to achieve sales goals.

These factors were critical in our experience selling cars. We maintain a healthy turnover and don't have an aged problem. Furthermore, you cannot be afraid to invest money into advertising your products and services. You have to be everywhere. Whether it's TV, radio, social media, or Internet search, you must maintain a significant presence. Multiply your efforts by ten here and you will reap the rewards. I knew that, if I was going to have a 20 percent close ratio, I simply needed more customers. Increase traffic and know what your staff will do with that increase. While the customers are coming in, invest your energy in improving your process, and watch your close ratio grow with the increased traffic. When your sales volume goes up, don't try to save yourselves by trying incessantly to maximize profits. I see a lot of dealers get scared and do this. Dominate the market; don't compete. With your follow-up tools on autopilot, as mine are, your goal must be to get your customers to come back. With increased growth, your space will need to grow and, therefore, forecasting increased sales needs to include increased staff and space. If you don't have space, make space. That action has been crucial in our expansion to become the top dealer at a single location in Austin, TX.

Sales Execution

What do you imagine when you think about sales execution? Simply defined, execution is simply another term for making the sale. This entire book is about making the sale, but there are several reasons why I'm including an entire section about execution specifically. First, the difference between simply talking about sales, which we're doing throughout this book, and executing the sales, which we do on the sales floor, is huge. It's the difference between theory and practice. Ask any successful practitioner how big of a difference there is between theory and practice and he'll tell you it's big.

Does this mean that all the theory discussed in previous chapters was a waste? Absolutely not. In fact, that knowledge becomes even more valuable since it becomes the basis of and the rationale for our actions.

Another reason we need to study about sales execution is, when you implement theoretical ideas into practice, you come face to face with the problems and the difficulties of such an endeavor. I can provide you with a general outlook of what the sales process looks like and what to do and what to avoid. But since every process is different, and every circumstance is different, the problems that arise as a result of each process are also different. There can also be a wide range of practical solutions to a problem, which we must take into account as well.

Sales execution, as you likely understand by now, is the way in which we implement the sales process we've created through daily practice. It involves the trials and tribulations of customer care. It concerns the rigors and rewards of achieving monthly targets. It relates to the failures and frustrations of selling your product. Sales execution is the moment of truth. It demonstrates your knowledge about the product, tests the viability of the process, and proves the worthiness of the people. All fancy terminologies, rules of procedure, advice, and suggestions lead up to this. It is the end point. And, in a way, it is also the beginning—the beginning of the difficult road ahead, the uncharted territory into which we all must venture at one point or another.

But we don't set out blindly. We have a set of rules and tools to guide us. So let's examine some of these rules of sales execution.

My 10 Commandments of Sales

HAVE A POSITIVE ATTITUDE

You must have a positive attitude that will rub off on your customers. Your energy will transfer. If you've had zero sales in the first ten days of the month, don't let your attitude meet your disappointment, Remember, in the last few days of the month you may end up having 25 sales in a row!

BE CONFIDENT THAT YOU CAN SELL TO ANYONE

No matter what the customer's appearance when he walks into the dealership, many salespeople don't exude a quiet confidence. The customer sees that and infers that the salesperson is new and, therefore, doesn't wish to work with him.

KNOW YOUR PRODUCT

You have to know the product you're trying to sell, inside and out. Review brochures, go through all of the technology, drive the car, read up on the features and benefits, and know the highlights of each vehicle.

BE SOLD ON THE PRODUCT YOU'RE SELLING

If you aren't sold on the product you're selling, you need to get out of the business. Wherever you go to work, it's imperative that you're sold on the *brand* that you're selling day-in and day-out. Don't work for a dealership where you can't get excited about the product.

Think about a product you believe in. Now think about one you don't. Which could you sell more of, more genuinely, with more excitement?

MAKE SURE YOU HAVE THE RIGHT TOOLS

Make sure you have a working computer, software, a sharpened pencil, pen with ink, etc. If you have a glitch, it's a disruption of the process. You have to be efficient. Not having a pen makes you seem flighty, and it breaks confidence with the customer.

DRESS TO IMPRESS

In short, look professional. Sometimes salespeople come to work in wrinkled shirts, not mentally prepared, shirt untucked, and wearing dirty shoes. At our dealership everyone has to be in a uniform or wearing a tie. You must feel professional because you *are* professional.

HAVE GOOD HYGIENE

Take a shower. Brush your teeth. Wear deodorant. Don't wear too much cologne. The customer has to want to be around you!

KNOW YOUR INVENTORY

You should be regularly walking your inventory so that you know where all cars are parked. We have 1500 cars in stock, on average, and I know essentially where each of them is. Don't waste time looking for a car when a customer wants a specific vehicle. Know the general area in which the each car is stored in order to save time.

BE AWARE OF YOUR SURROUNDINGS

Being aware of your surroundings is critical. Oftentimes, salespeople will be sitting in a corner talking to one another when they should be attuned to what's going on around them—when a customer walks in, through which entrance he enters, etc. Oftentimes, there are back or side entrances, and you'd be surprised how often customers enter through them. Customers should not be standing in the showroom with no one taking care of them because no one noticed them. It's unprofessional.

HAVE GREAT WORKING RELATIONSHIPS WITH EVERY DEPARTMENT, SALES-SERVICE-BUSINESS OFFICE-FINANCE

You have to be able to talk to everyone in the office—from sales to service to finance—because everyone has to want to help you sell as many vehicles as you can. People rarely understand that there are referrals within the business as well; co-workers will send you their family and friends when they learn that they are in the market for a new vehicle.

Critical Considerations When Executing Car Sales

It all starts with a vision—a vision to succeed, to achieve sales targets, to take your dealership beyond what other dealerships even dream of. But, as the saying goes, vision without execution is just hallucination. According to another saying, execution without vision is a nightmare. The two go hand-in-hand. One cannot survive without the other. So these are two key areas on which you need to focus. And, incidentally, these are two areas where car dealerships make the most mistakes. Either the vision is wrong to begin with, or there are serious errors in execution. But, there are ways to avoid that.

Let's begin with the vision. This is the first and foremost prerequisite for successful sales execution. Without it, there's no chance of achieving your sales target. You might do it, but it would be a fluke. In any case, how exactly can we define and come up with a vision? Some people are just born leaders. They have a unique outlook on what they want to achieve. A vision comes easily to them. Those who are successfully capable of capitalizing on that vision go on to become market leaders, millionaires, billionaires, CEOs, or entrepreneurs.

What if you are not a born leader? What if you have no clue about car sales? Can a vision be acquired? It certainly can be. You can learn to be a successful businessperson or a sales manager. Many people have done so. They are continuing to push the boundaries of what they can achieve in sales. And, if you ask these people how they acquired the perfect sales vision, none of them would say it came to him overnight. It just doesn't happen that way. A vision begins with a seed—the germ of an idea, a rudimentary goal.

In this case, the goal is plain and simple. Sell 1000 cars per month. That's the germ of an idea. It's the bare bones of your sales strategy. You build your vision around it. You put the meat on the bones. You begin with the thought of drastically increasing your sales targets. Then you find a team to achieve that. Then you build a process for your team to follow. Then you work hard on perfecting the process. One step at a time, you gradually build your vision. But not everyone can do it.

Anyone can think of selling a thousand cars a month, but few know how best to do it. Even fewer will be able to successfully follow through on that vision.

When it comes to successfully executing the sales plan, you need to know that it'll be hard. Mistakes will occur. You will need to go through a rigorous trial and error process. You will make changes to your original vision. You will step back, step forward, backtrack, and move ahead. You will learn to never be afraid of making mistakes. Theodore Roosevelt said, "The only man who never makes a mistake is the man who never does anything." If you want to sell 1000 cars, you must be prepared to make mistakes and learn from them.

THREE STAGES OF A SALES EXECUTION MODEL

The biggest problem you may encounter in perfecting sales execution is, you won't know where or how to start. Many sales people find it overwhelming to even begin. Granted, it's a daunting task. But it seems all the more challenging when you look at the whole picture. The way that works best for me is, rather than looking at the bigger picture, I think about each component of the sales execution process, and consider how it can contribute to the bigger picture. It's easy if you think about it—focusing on one step at a time is much easier than focusing on everything at once.

Imagine you were given the task of building the pyramids in Egypt. Where would you even begin? The pyramids are huge. No matter how much effort you put in to the thought, you might never get around to actually doing the building. Look at it this way, however: building a pyramid is hard. It's almost unachievable. But laying a brick is easy. Anyone can do it. So why not think about laying bricks instead of building pyramids. How simple it is when you think about it like that. Place one brick at a time each and every day. It will likely be slightly confusing at first. The bricks will look like in a random formation, and there may be no method to the madness. But as you carry on, brick by brick, you will begin to see the shape of a pyramid emerge. You'll know where to go. And even if you don't manage to finish it in your lifetime, others can build upon your framework.

Setting out to improve sales execution is similar. Selling 1000 cars per month is hard. But hiring a competent sales person is relatively easy. Small though it may be, it is an action that brings you one step closer to success. Your task as a manager is to constantly take baby steps every day. By the end of the month, you will feel better about your efforts. By the end of the quarter, you'll see a visible rise in the numbers. By the end of the year, you'll look back and be surprised at how you managed to come this far. If you want to perfect your sales execution, break down the bigger task of selling 1000 cars per month into a series of smaller tasks. If you want to come up with an ideal sales execution model, consider the process as having three key stages.

1. Pre-sales execution
2. Sales execution
3. Post-sales execution

All these stages come under the umbrella of sales execution in general. Let's consider them one at a time.

PRE-SALES EXECUTION

Your sales execution model comes into play long before the sales process begins. This is the pre-sales phase, and it's crucial for the success of the actual sales process. This is the stage where you translate your vision into an achievable set of goals. A lot of thought must go into the pre-sales execution in order to enable you to achieve your targets. It's not as simple as it sounds, however. The pre-sales phase does not simply involve sitting in contemplation of what may come ahead. It involves taking practical measures to prepare yourself, your team, and your process for what's about to happen on the sales floor. These practical measures can be a part of any one of the pre-sales processes.

RESEARCH

Your success as a sales manager largely depends upon how informed you are. Are you prepared to crunch the numbers? If not, you should be. Research is the starting point of any successful sales strategy. It's a process through which you find out the facts that matter. From reading this book to going out in the field and assessing the competition, research has many facets. You need to first see where you actually stand in comparison to your competition. You need to gauge market conditions. You need to set competitive prices for your products while also retaining healthy profit margins.

Your research illuminates the path that lies ahead. It enables you to make healthy decisions. If you research, you basically know the consequences of your actions before you take them. While an unseen force may occasionally influence the outcome, you must know where you are going and how you will get there. Beyond market research, your customer research is important as well. What are the current consumer trends? Which vehicles are most popular with the customers? What's the buyer demographic? Your research isn't complete without answers to these questions.

PLAN

This is where all the sales theory that you've learned from this book comes into play. This is also the stage that requires the most amount of thought. Since you must follow a pre-planned strategy to ensure smooth functioning of sales, you need to invest in a fair amount of planning. This is the drawing board stage. It's the part of the process where you figure out in which direction you want to take your sales team. You also plan based on your research results. Whatever data you have, figure out the best way to use it to your advantage. That's planning.

The most important component of planning is coming up with the process. I've already dedicated a chapter to creating the sales process since it is one of the most important things to do before you even set foot on the sales floor. Your process precedes your actions and, in a way, dictates them as well. Your process is the backbone of your sales, the foundation upon which the entire whole structure stands. All the research and thought you invested toward coming up with the strategy manifest in the sales process you create.

PREPARE

What exactly is the difference between planning and preparation? Aren't they two different words for the exact same thing? Not quite. Planning is fleshing out the sales process. Preparation is actively taking practical steps in pursuance of that process. These are steps just short of sales, steps that lead up to the sales. Preparation is significant since it determines whether or not your sales will succeed. The better prepared you are, the better your chances will be to become a successful sales person, achieving the monthly target of selling 1000 cars.

One of the most important pre-sales steps is building the team. You need to find the right people, and train them well. When hiring, there are a few critical points to consider. First, and this one's a no-brainer, your team must be talented. No matter how much training you provide to your staff, if they don't have that unique quality that makes them good salespersons, your efforts will be wasted. Second, even if they're not qualified enough, as long as they have that fire and that passion to succeed, bring them on board. Qualification is not everything. Third, and most importantly, you must pay your sales people more than what your competitors are paying. Good salaries create a brain drain and attract the best talents to a company. They're often the difference between success and failure.

SALES EXECUTION

Now that you have crunched the numbers, come up with a plan, and hired the right team, it's time to gear up and start moving full-speed in the right direction. It's time to execute the sales. This is inarguably the most important aspect of sales since it involves the actual sales itself. This is why we have given it the most attention in previous chapters. By this point, you have been fairly well-educated on ways to improve your sales number. Now it's time to consider how you can execute that entire process.

Once, you manage to gather a team of hard-working dedicated salespeople, it becomes time to gauge their performance. It's time to "inspect what you expect." This phrase has stuck with me since my first management job years ago. This is the time when you help get your people from 10-cars-a-month players to 15- to 20-cars-a-month players. This is where you have to make sure you "turn every customer." We preach this philosophy to each one of our team players. We ask them not to pressure a customer but instead to simply discover why we couldn't sell him a car. This will help you identify where your salespeople need help.

The floor manager plays a crucial role in this step. Make sure you increase your manager's objectives, not only in terms of sales but also in their close ratios. You have to know the numbers. You need effective division of labor. Assign your business development (BDC) managers to web leads and phone calls and floor managers to walk-in customers. Your sales managers are accountable for everything. Push your people toward greatness. Ask your managers to set an example for your salespeople through consummate professionalism and brilliant performance.

I recently read *The Sell* by Fredrik Eklund, and he has a great motto: "Train like a prizefighter." When you work had on your sales team and they begin to deliver, that is when you come to understand how great they truly are. Don't forget to appreciate their performance. It requires consistent action to get your team to perform at the top of their game every time. If you don't constantly push them to do more and encourage them to perform better, they will revert back to old habits. You have to continue to sell your people on the vision and the dream. When everyone is working together, that's where greatness occurs. "Team work makes the dream work." You must remember that.

The Oxford Dictionary defines education as "the carrying out of a plan, order, or course of action." This is the plan you must work on to increase your action every day. Just as in any major sporting event—consider the Olympics, for instance—the athletes train every day. They practice. They rehearse the plays. When it's time, they execute. The same goes for sales. If you want to be a professional, you have to continue to learn, grow, hustle, grind, and repeat.

It's the cycle. It's what has made me more money than I could ever have dreamed. You must teach your people, and help them grow. I like the saying "If you want to be a billionaire, then figure out how to help a billion people." I'm not going to tell you that you'll be a billionaire by selling 1000 cars per moth, but I've seen salespeople in our industry make anywhere from $300,000 to $1,000,000 per year. Of course, there are even bigger fish in the sea. There are richer salespersons like Van Tuyl, who recently sold 78 of his dealerships to Warren Buffet for just over $4 billion. So, I guess it *is* possible.

POST-SALES EXECUTION

If you ask a sales representative what the sales execution process looks like, most of them will describe the actual sales process in action. Some will even go as far as to include some pre-sales activities, such as building a team, into their sales execution vision. But few will actually include the post-sales activities into the mix. That's how little attention these activities receive. If you ask the customer, however, which part of the sales process made the most lasting impression on him and compelled him to visit the dealership again, he would likely point toward many of the post-sales activities. That's how crucial these activities are.

If we set out to explore why there's such a huge difference between the actual and perceived importance of post-sales execution, we will find many answers. Maybe the sales representatives don't imagine post-sales execution as being a part of their job. Maybe they don't feel that it makes much of a difference with the customer. Maybe they find it dull and boring. All of these answers seem to be divergent paths, but these paths lead to the same destination. All of these questions have a single answer: we must improve our post-sales executions if we want to find repeat business and increase our monthly sales.

What exactly are some of the post-sales activities? How can we work on these activities to improve post-sales execution? To answer these questions, a precise definition of post-sales activities is in order. Post-sales activities are the interactions with sold customers or the analysis of past sales. These are the activities that don't directly lead to or prepare for sales. But the indirect impact they may have is enormous. For instance, gathering customer feedback, follow-up with sold customers, sales evaluation, and analysis are all examples of post-sales activities. Once we clearly identify these activities, it's time to move forward.

If you are a salesperson, the activities that are of most interest to you must be the ones where you interact directly with the customers. For sales managers, these activities also include evaluating sales trends and comparing your sales numbers with your competitors. For an effective evaluation, you need customer feedback, so these activities go hand-in-hand. It's the manager's job to guide the sales representative as far as what information to obtain from the customer.

Effective communication between the sales hierarchies ensures an element of coherency in the process. Since sales are a constant process of continuous improvement, you need data on what you did wrong, for instance, in your most recent 10 follow-up calls. Once you have all the data, it's easier to identify patterns that can be modified to suit your sales process. This is one aspect of post-sales execution.

The other, more crucial, aspect of this process relates to the customers themselves. What do the customers think of their experiences with your dealership? How do they think it could be improved? If given a chance, would they shop again with you? Are they satisfied with their current vehicle? These questions are critical not only in terms of improving your dealership's rating on the Customer Satisfaction Index (CSI) but also for continuously revamping your sales process. The post-sale activities, in conjunction with the other two aforementioned sales activities, make up your sales execution model.

STEPS TO PERFECT SALES EXECUTION

Now that you know how to improve your sales execution, it's time to deliver a few finishing touches. With these steps, you will be able to polish your sales execution to perfection.

MAKE THE PERFECT TEAM

Building a team is the first step the sales execution. Building the right team is the only way you can perfect your sales execution. There's no need to go into the details of how important team building is, so let's jump right into how to make a perfect team. The process of building a team begins with trying to find talented people who help you achieve your monthly sales targets. But where do you find these talented people? The search begins within. Look into your own organization. Are there any rising stars? Are there any people in other departments who have an aptitude for sales? If so, these individuals should be your first choice.

Referrals are also a helpful way of finding new talent. Your existing employees are a great resource for finding potential salespeople they know. They are also a natural starting point in your quest for talent. Another avenue is networking in car sales circles. Hiring acquaintances is always a better option than posting for jobs and hiring strangers. But don't ignore that step. Sometimes, you may discover gems where you least expect them. Only once you have a team of talented professionals can you consider moving forward with your sales execution plan.

ADOPT A DATA-DRIVEN APPROACH

How do you expect to find the right sales approach if you don't even have the right tools at hand to go about it? Your data illuminates the path forward. It helps you stay on the right track. Remember to have lots of data. Imagine the process of sales execution as similar to navigating a foggy, murky swamp. It's difficult to navigate, and you don't know where you are going. When you realize you've set out on the wrong path, it may already be too late. The more data you have, the less murky the swamp will be. You will be able to clearly see the path ahead. And, even if you steer off path for a while, it's easy to realize that you're off-course and even easier to get back on the right path. Don't get lost in the sales haze; have lots of data in hand.

Your sales data can relate to your existing sales numbers. It may also include the analysis of previous sales statistics. You need to have data on your competitors; data on the market in general; records of customer feedback; a living, breathing customer database; all the product information; and the current car sales trends. All of this may seem overwhelming now, but it's easier once you break it down. Having all this data makes it easier for you to control the situation and skillfully maneuver around it or mold it in your favor.

TAILOR YOUR PROCESS TO THE BUYER'S NEEDS

Your sales process may be ingenious in the way it functions. It may be smooth, and one step may lead naturally to another. It may even feel like heaven for your sales staff. But the real question is, is the process a good fit for your customers' needs? How do you know whether customers are happy with your sales process? It's easy—you ask them! Constant feedback reins you in. It removes your limits. It tells you what to do and what to avoid.

If you want to tailor your sales process to the buyer's needs, three considerations are essential. First, don't make sales look like sales. Artful salespeople know how to accomplish this. Although they are selling a product just like you are, their customers are not actively aware that they are being sold a product simply for the sake of profit. Second, you need to constantly interact with the customer. Sales require two-way communication. You must get back more than you give. Third, you need effective communication not just between salespeople but also between upper management and other departments such as marketing and IT. With constant communication and a steady pool of knowledge, you will have enough information to go on. If you implement these three steps, you'll easily be able to tailor your sales process according to the buyer's needs.

REVIEW, REVISE, REASSESS, REPEAT

Once you have the team, the data, the customer feedback, and the will to succeed, it's time to look back on the sales process. How far have you come in terms of reaching your sales targets? What have you achieved in terms of improving your sales performance? What more can you do in terms of improving the sales execution? These are questions you need to ask periodically. The answers to these questions will determine how you move forward. Your sales execution process is never perfect. It needs constant revision.

Set up regular intervals to review your sales performance. Crunch the numbers and, if you are where you want to be, your sales execution is working perfectly. If not, you need a strategy to revise your sales execution model. How will you know what steps you need to change, eliminate, or add? For that, you need to reassess your entire sales strategy. Carefully analyze each and every step. Refer to your dataset again and again. Find weaknesses or gaps or cracks in the structure, and identify a way to repair these cracks. Once you do that, you know what to do to improve your sales process.

DON'T BE AFRAID OF FAILURE

Thomas Edison once said, "Many of life's failures are people who did not realize how close they were to success when they gave up." This is a profound statement, one that left a deep impact on my heart. Not only is it true for life in general, it is applicable to any sphere of professional activity. If you decide to commit to the goal of selling 1000 cars per month, you must fully commit. You will fail. Not once, not twice—many times. It's not about how many times you fall. It's about how many times you pick yourself up after you fall. That's the path that leads to success.

When you set out on the journey, don't be afraid of failure. Your path will be difficult. Failure will haunt you, and success will elude you, but not for long if you follow the aforementioned steps and are diligent. You need to be relentless in your approach. So what if you fail? So what if something you come up with doesn't work? So what if you lose some customers? They'll come back. You simply need to stand back up on your feet every time you fall.

Don't Compete. Dominate.

When we entered the Austin, Texas, marketplace 5 years ago with Charles Maund Toyota, my General Manager had a simple plan: we had to become the number one dealership in the area. It did indeed seem simple at the time. All we had to do was to keep track of our competitors, know what they were doing, and beat them at every step by matching their efforts. Knowing their every move in advance, we could plan ours. I imagined it to be like a chess match—a constant back and forth between us and our competitors. How wrong I was. It takes a lot to be number one and a whole lot more to stay number one.

A time came when I had become increasingly disillusioned with traditional models of competition. They simply weren't yielding positive results, and it felt like going down the rabbit hole each time. We were stuck in a constant, predictable loop. We couldn't increase the sales numbers beyond a particular level. It was frustrating, and we didn't know what to do. But everything changed when I read Cardone's advice: "Don't compete. Dominate." It was simple and succinct, yet it carried a lot of weight. It opened new doors for me and for our dealership. I'm now at a point where I work 6 days a week, and it doesn't feel like I'm working.

How can such a simple statement be so profound? What exactly are the implications of this statement? These are fascinating questions, and they are a good place to start if you're absolutely clueless as well as a good place to regroup if you've lost your way. By thoroughly analyzing the meaning behind "Don't Compete. Dominate," we find a wealth of information that can propel us further in our journey to success and our plans to sell 1000 cars per month.

When you attempt to dominate the market, you need to drill your message into everyone's heads. Everyone needs to know that you are the only dealership from which to buy. A prominent example of this is the way that Coca Cola markets its products. To say they've been successful is a gross understatement. The impact of their marketing strategy was that that today, when customers ask for a soda, they ask for a "Coke." The message is drilled into their subconscious. It's a part of their identity to the point that they don't have to stop and reconsider when buying a coke. That's how you dominate the market. That's how you become the market. And that's the only way to survive. Don't simply compete with others. Be so big that others fear competing with you. That should be your sales philosophy. This is how you'll keep selling 1000 cars per month and stay ahead of your competition at all times. This is how you'll become (and remain) number one.

How to Dominate the Car Sales Market

Whether you're a new dealership in town or an old one trying to regain lost glory, you need to make an effort to dominate the market. Although this is a challenge even under normal circumstances, it becomes even more of one when you consider the current economic crises. The recession is destroying everything in its path. Businesses are scrambling for ways to stay afloat. They're scraping the bottom of the barrel, clinging hopelessly for survival. It's a storm that's raising all the ships and bringing them down hard, smashing them into bits. That's the kind of environment you enter when you go in to dominate. Not only do you have to swim against the tide, you need to rise above the rest of the swimmers.

What should you do if you're stuck in such a situation? Conventional wisdom dictates that you must be protective. Cut down on costs, limit your operations, lay of excess staff, find economic means to run your business, save, conserve, and limit yourself. Some of these tactics are helpful, essential even. But do we need to limit ourselves in a recession? Many successful salespeople believe that recession is not a time to contract, but instead to expand. It's not a time to implode but instead to explode with all your might. It's not a time to hide your cards but instead to go all in.

During economic implosions, the natural tendency of organizations and individuals is to respond by shrinking—this is a mistake! Implosions are the time to advance, conquer and take market share from those that elect to retreat. Now is the time to separate yourself from everyone in your sector through your actions. The only way to survive and prosper when things around you are contracting is to expand and it is impossible to expand while contracting."

If you decide to risk an expansion, what do you expand into? Where do you spend most of your money? During a financial crisis, your business savings are twice as valuable for your survival. Spending these savings on any activity is twice as risky. So, naturally, you need to be four times as careful with regard to where to spend your money. Therefore, these are my recommended steps to help you achieve your goal of dominating the market:

DON'T BE AFRAID TO SPEND MONEY

If you're prepared to dominate the market, you need to spend more money on marketing than you usually would. That's the rule of thumb. There's no other way. You can choose to either save your money or save the position of the market leader for yourself. There are two ways of looking at the money you spend on marketing. The first is as "spending" and the second is as "investment." If you think of the money as the former, you're less likely to spend more and more likely to cut it down when your business faces troubled times.

The best way to look at the money you spend on marketing is as an investment—a long-term investment that doesn't yield immediate returns but will make the difference between life and death when it comes to your business's survival. Thinking that way makes it easier for you to commit more money to marketing and more difficult to cut down when you believe that you need to. The future of your business hinges upon how much you spend. It will be expensive for the first two or so years, but once your business establishes itself and finds firm ground and a healthy client base, you'll begin to see steady returns on that investment.

While spending more is important, spending smart is even more important. Don't just think about how much you spend, think about where you spend it. Think about how best to spend what you have. This is where conventional business notions of being economical can be addressed. Being economical doesn't mean spending less. Instead, it means making the most of what you can spend. Don't be afraid to spend more, but when you do, make sure it counts.

BEAT COMPETITORS' PRICES

When we entered the business, we knew we had to make some compromises to be number one and stay there. We had to "take the good with the bad." If that meant beating someone's price, that's what we had to do. This is the one basic rule of competition and the one thing that almost anyone can do. It is something you need to be the best at. Don't give your competitors a chance to steal your customers by offering lower prices. Beat their prices on every product, every offer, every step of the way. You should be prepared to match everything they offer. Only when you know your competitors' every move can you stay one step ahead.

If you read this and are thinking about waging an all-out price war, you're gravely mistaken. Competing on prices is like walking on thin ice—one crack and you're down under. One misstep and your business will freeze. In a price war, there's only one victor. If you're not the dealership with the lowest prices, you will lose most of your customers. However, if you stretch the profit margins to the absolute thinnest, you can only run so far with them. You won't be able to sustain them for long. And when you go down, your business will go down with you.

The best way is to find a path that offers you a way to compete is to dominate your competitors without harming your own business. Use price competition in combination with a multitude of other strategies. If you make price your only selling point, you're doomed to fail. If you want to succeed, don't go all out on price, but don't ignore it either. This is the first step in the great game of market domination.

182 | CHRIS MARTINEZ

Make sure you play your cards right. You cannot afford to lose here.

ADVERTISE AGGRESSIVELY

Have you seen a brand that dominates the market but doesn't advertise aggressively? You haven't, because there's no such brand. It is physically impossible. Remember the Coca Cola example? You have to drill your message into the buyers' heads. You need to penetrate their subconscious. That's only possible through excessive advertising. You may hear sales experts denouncing aggressive advertising and asking businesses to avoid it like the plague. But that's precisely why you'll succeed. Since no one goes down that route, it's free for the taking. Aggressive advertising, if executed correctly, can work wonders for your organization.

You need to be smart in your approach when it comes to advertising. Avoid being tedious, boring, too repetitive and, most of all, annoying. Find that balance. Find ways to be smart about your advertising. When the path forward is littered with challenges, you have to be creative, and advertising provides you with a multitude of opportunities to creatively get your message across. If you have fun with your marketing strategies, it won't seem as tedious, boring, or annoying as conventional advertising.

When it comes to advertising, the most important underlying condition is that you must have something to advertise. You have to find that unique selling point that no one else can offer. This is easier in general retail than in car sales. Retailers can easily come up with a unique product, and their product is their selling point. Car dealerships don't have that opportunity. If you're selling a Toyota Corolla, ten other dealerships in the area may be selling the exact same thing. There's not much space to maneuver on products. This is why you need to find other unique selling points. You have to come up with unconventional promotions, attractive discounts, and enticing offers. Those will be your selling points. If you have something unique to sell and you have a unique way of selling it, your advertising plan will be successful.

USE EVERY MEDIA OUTLET

Another way to succeed in advertising is to maintain a steady presence on all "increase your action" media channels. Apply the philosophy here. Whether conventional channels such as TV, print, and radio or newer channels like social media and the digital landscape, your goal is to be visible. Your demographic is spread unevenly across all spaces, and you need to reach everyone. That's why you have to have a presence in every media outlet. You cannot pick and choose based on your preferences. So what if you don't listen to the radio? So what if you think print is obsolete? Your audience determines the channels you choose. And since you want to dominate the market, you have to reach all the audiences.

When you consider using every media outlet, you must come up with a unique strategy for every channel. I have seen many businesses repurpose their content. They shoot an ad for TV, play the same in radio, and print the transcript in the local newspaper. That is the definition of lazy, and the fact is that the audience expectations for every medium are widely divergent. A TV ad needs to be engaging, a newspaper ad needs to be visually stimulating, and for radio, your ad must be creative enough to capture the listener's imagination. Your strategy for these mediums must be unique.

Data is your friend while you're forming a marketing strategy for different media channels. You must do your research to determine the best times to reach your audiences, specifically potential buyers. The best way to capture hot leads is to market during programs during which the most viewers and listeners are expected to buy vehicles. For instance, auto shows on TV and radio are your best bets. Auto magazines in print are also a good way to reach your audience.

IMPROVE DIGITAL MARKETING

Nearly two-thirds of Americans use social media. Statistics suggest that a staggering 90 percent of young Americans have an account on at least one social media channel. With so many of potential customers online, it's a no-brainer to suggest reliance on digital marketing if you want to dominate the market. Surprisingly, however, many in the car sales industry have failed to realize that. They continue to rely on traditional means of advertising that, although important in their own right, fail to yield the desired results.

If you want to dominate the car sales market, you must first dominate the social media and other digital platforms. If you want to sell 1000 cars per month, your digital marketing strategy must be on-point. This isn't hard if you're willing to get into the nitty-gritty of it, but it does demand your full, undivided attention. Perhaps this is why many car dealerships shy away from entering the digital marketing landscape. But their reluctance provides you with a valuable opportunity to capitalize on the absence of many of your competitors from social media.

To do that, you need a social media strategy. Building a social media strategy from the ground up is a systematic process, not unlike building a sales process. It begins with gathering data on which you build the foundation of what's to come. You then need to begin to create a strategy tailored to the needs of the customers and the requirements of your marketing campaign. It's a step-by-step process. You begin by targeting the two most dominant social media channels, Facebook and Twitter. You continue to expand to other channels in order to reach out to wider audiences. This is one direction in which your social media strategy evolves.

Another direction in which it expands is the scope of your marketing campaign. While embarking on the creation of a social media strategy, you can begin with a small home-run campaign targeting a limited number of people focusing on a limited number of social media activities. However, as your strategy continues to expand, you may require the services of digital marketing campaign experts. You may also need to spend more on online advertising. As the scope of your digital marketing campaign expands, so will your customer base.

But remember, your goal is not just to expand your customer base. It is to dominate the market. This is why you need to be relentless in creating a social media marketing strategy. Observe what your competitors are doing, and perform ten times the action, invest ten times the energy, and perhaps invest ten times the money as well.

SEARCH ENGINE OPTIMIZATION (SEO)

The first step on the journey to forming an online presence is creating a website. Since most customers now search the internet before stepping out of their houses to buy a vehicle, you need an all-purpose website that enables potential customers to view your inventory and learn about your promotional offers. What if you find out after investing hard work into the creation of the website that it's simply not visible on the search engines? Search engines are responsible for directing the highest amount of traffic to your website. Therefore, simply creating a website is not enough these days. You need to improve the website's visibility on the search engines as well.

For that, you need Search Engine Optimization (SEO). To optimize your website for maximum search engine visibility, you first need to know the search terms that people type into search engines when looking for vehicles. When you analyze the kinds of search queries people use, you can classify them into the following three categories:

NAVIGATIONAL SEARCH

When you imagine searching a company or service online, this is considered navigational research, and it is one of the most common types of Google searches. It is also the one that brings some of the most valuable prospects to your website. These are the people who know about your company or brand. Why else would anyone search for Charles Maund Toyota in Texas if they hadn't already heard about it? To optimize your website for navigational searches, you must have a unique brand name so that your website doesn't get lost in a slew of other similarly-named business websites.

INFORMATIONAL SEARCH

An informational search is one in which the prospect searches for general information on a topic. For instance, if someone types in "where to find the best cars in Texas," that would be considered an informational search. When optimizing your website for informational searches, you need to produce quality content, and lots of it. Search engines demand quality, and they promote the website that provides value to the reader. Is your website capable of delivering to both demands? If not, you need to figure out ways to produce more quality content that focuses on meeting customers' demands rather than selling products. You also need to conduct research on some of the most common queries that customers use to conduct an informational search about your product. You need to select some of the most important keywords, and deliver quality content built around those keywords.

TRANSACTIONAL SEARCH

This is the kind of search that's conducted by super-hot leads. These are ready-to-buy customers who have both money in their pockets and the willingness to step out of their homes to purchase your products. Some of these search queries may include "best car dealerships in Austin, Texas" or "Toyota car prices in Austin, Texas." Optimizing your website for transactional search is relatively more difficult than for navigational or informational searches. Google uses graph results to conduct side-by-side product and price comparisons.

Your website needs to have an encoded markup that allows Google's algorithm to pick up product and price details to display in its search results.

SEARCH ENGINE MARKETING (SEM)

Although SEO and SEM are related terms and sometimes used interchangeably, there's a big difference between search engine optimization and search engine marketing. The difference is denoted by organic versus paid results. Let's suppose potential buyers in your area search for car prices and see two kinds of links in the search results. The organic results are the ones that the search engine naturally brings up to assist the customers in their query. Sponsored links are those that are featured prominently on the top of the search results. Search engine marketing involves paying the search engines to display your content so that you receive more traffic.

You need to tread carefully here. It might be tempting to continue advertising your website in order to gain the lion's share of traffic. The return on investment in SEM can, sometimes, be surprisingly high. But it can also be temporary. Regular spending on SEM can put a strain on your wallet, and as soon as you pull out to save money, your website traffic falls more quickly than you might realize. This is why it's important not to rely on SEM too much, and always focus more of your energy on SEO to create an organic following. Search engine marketing can help you break into the market, but you're on your own after that.

There are various techniques to improve your SEM game. The most common among them is the pay per click (PPC) model. As the name suggests, PPC advertising is one in which you pay the search engine a fixed sum of money for each visitor who comes to your website through the sponsored link. This kind of advertising may be beneficial for you since you pay for the actual number of visitors to your website. On the other, it may open you up to abuse or click fraud—a situation where your competitors or someone with malicious intent generates website clicks and leaves you paying the price (literally) without receiving any customers.

CUSTOMER RETENTION

You cannot even begin to think about dominating the market if you don't work on customer retention. Retention is a measure of how loyal your existing customers are to your business. When setting out to conquer the marketplace, your existing customers are your biggest resource. If you cannot retain your customers, you won't be able to capture the market, no matter how hard you try. Like holding a fistful of sand, you will never quite manage to hold on to it for long. That's why it's essential to close one end of the funnel.

The way to achieve that is simple: conduct a follow-up. A good follow-up is the key to customer retention. Coming up with the idea of a follow-up may be simple, but successfully conducting it is hard. However, the task can be made significantly easier through customer retention software. I use theautominer.com for the job. It helps me hone in on my previous customers and keep them coming back. You have to keep a track of customer preferences, give each and every customer a unique treatment, make him feel special, follow his schedule, and contact him regularly. All of this can be overwhelming without a program to manage the various tasks.

Even with the assistance of the software, you are the one who must perform the bulk of the work. You must actually interact with the customer to bring him back. The responsibility falls on you and your team, and you must step up to the task. Here are some of the ways you can do that:

Deliver a great product at affordable price: This is the first rule of getting your customers to return. Simply deliver a better price and product than your competitors, and your customers will return. This step is so important that no matter how much attention you pay to customer service and developing personal relationships with your customers, at the end of the day they'll choose the dealership that offers them the best deal. Conversely, even if your customer service has slight shortcomings, you can still win over your customers. And, since most car dealerships offer more or less the same quality products, the price must be a critical component of your focus.

Deliver good customer service: Good customer service is the basic requirement for selling automobiles, or for selling any product, really. Why, then, did I feel the need to mention or elaborate on it? It should go without saying, right? Wrong. This is exactly the mindset that sales managers should avoid. Delivering good customer service is so obvious that, sometimes, some dealerships take it for granted and, in their haste to move on to other steps, skip this step entirely. Avoid this at all costs. Always deliver exceptional customer service. How many times have you heard the phrase "getting back to the basics"? Well, these are the basics, and you need to get back to them if you want to retain customers.

Focus on building personal relationships: What constitutes good customer service? is a common question among salespeople and, to us, no less valuable than a philosopher's quest to understand the meaning of life. But, unlike the philosophers, we have a definitive answer—or, at least a key part of the answer. Good customer service means building personal relationships with the customers. It means treating the customers as individuals rather than sales targets. It means respecting their humanity and showing them respect. That is the key to sales and the single most effective way to retain existing customers.

Stroke the customer's ego: When you set out to build human relationships, don't forget the purpose behind it—to dominate the sales market and sell 1000 cars per month. In order to do that, you need to have several sales tricks up your sleeves. One of those tricks is stroking the customer's ego. Every customer feels the need to be considered important. Every ego needs to be stroked. That's your job as a salesperson. If you do it well, you will get one step closer to your sales goals.

Reward your customers frequently: Sales is a process of reciprocity. It's a process of give and take. This reciprocity extends far beyond paying money and receiving the product. If a customer visits again, you should try to treat them better than you did during his earlier visit. Customers are apprehensive on their second visits. Although they chose to visit you again, they're not exactly sold on doing business with you again. Their second visit is the perfect opportunity for you to make them a long-term customer. You can also create specific programs to reward regular customers. VIP is the important word here. Customers love being considered special, or VIP. It adds an element of exclusivity, and VIP programs can go a long way in terms of ensuring customer loyalty.

---

7 Tactics to Advance and Conquer

TRAINING

You must ensure that your staff members are ninjas at selling. If you can continue to attract the same amount of traffic year after year but improve your closing ratio, you can sell more in every category: phone, email, social media, chat, walk-in, service, follow-up, data-mining and prospecting.

It's critical to be continuously training your salespeople through daily meetings, one-on-one training, etc. Make sure that training is an integral part of your dealership's culture.

ENSURE MARKETING DOLLARS ARE PRODUCING

Verify that every penny spent on marketing is working hard for you every single day. If you aren't on top of your marketing game, you're wasting money. As has been said, sinks ship because of the tiny holes—the ones that aren't noticed until they've let in too much water. I review our marketing efforts daily. We look at where we're spending money, what's working, what isn't working, where we need to pivot and what new marketing options we want to explore.

EVOLVE

Continue to identify new ways to reach your customers, and revisit and hone old methods as well. When dealerships reach the 500-cars-per-month mark, they must quickly figure out how to hire more people in order to reach 750-cars-per-month. It's critical to be proactively forward-thinking in terms of how you will continue to grow because if you get complacent, someone will take your business away from you. Consider where you can build a new lot, how you can expand your current lot, how you can hire new salespeople and how you can adjust your overall efforts in order to ensure that you don't lose customers to new dealerships.

CONQUER

Go after fans of every brand. I've known many Toyota dealerships that only want to go after the Toyota customer. It's critical to strategize in order to win other brand's customers.

SPEND SMART

Some dealerships create their budget with no solid basis. If you can spend additional money in a smart way to gain additional market share, take the risk. A great example is social media marketing. For a while, no one was spending money in this area. We created an additional budget for social media marketing so that we could go after a greater market share without reducing our budgets for TV and radio ads.

MAINTAIN YOUR REPUTATION

Maintaining a solid reputation is a full-time job. The main reason anyone is in business is to take care of customers. Anytime you forget that, you lose. Make sure you're doing everything possible to take care of your customers so that when they talk about you they say only good things and will spread the message about your dealership *for* you.

BE EVERYWHERE

Again, get out of obscurity. Be strategic and active on social media including Facebook, Instagram, LinkedIn and Twitter as well as radio, TV, print and mail. Consistency is key, so if you have to start with only two or three platforms in order to be consistent, it's better to take that approach than start with eight platforms haphazardly.

The Key to Customer Satisfaction: Treat People Right

There's an old saying: "Treat others the way you want to be treated." And this, in a way, sums up my entire sales philosophy, and it's critical to being able to sell 1000 cars per month. I usually wouldn't pay much heed to folk wisdom while creating a sales strategy. But, in this case, I'm willing to make an exception because of the significant value of treating people right. Not only does this have practical implications, it also helps you to be a happier person in the long term. Our goal is not to learn the secrets of living a happier life. Other people have written much more eloquently and authoritatively on that subject. Our job is to sell cars, and lots of them.

How we behave in order to sell cars is as important as actually selling those cars, if not more so. Increasing sales numbers is the ultimate goal, but the nature of our means to do so determines the nature of the end result. This means that how we go about increasing those sales numbers dictates the outcome. I have observed may salespeople who claim they are "the real deal" make such egregious mistakes when it comes to treating the customers that I couldn't help but cringe. It's the solely numbers-oriented sales approach that ruins a customer's buying experience. And it's those hot-shot salespeople considering themselves above the needs of their customers who give our profession a bad name.

A good salesperson should be, above all, humble. Egoism and self-importance is the sales equivalent of pushing an organization downstairs. If you want to succeed in sales, you need to treat all your customers like millionaires. It doesn't matter if you're a celebrity sales person or if other sales people come to you for advice. From the customer's perspective, you're just there to assist them in the sales process. You have no identity other than that of a facilitator. If you do that job right, the customers will likely remember your face. They are the elite. They deserve the "Ritz Carlton" experience. They require your full attention.

There's no set way of treating people right. Sometimes it can be as simple as taking off your sunglasses, removing the Bluetooth earpiece, or turning off your phone. At other times, it can be a more intricate task such as remembering each and every one of the customer's particular demands, maintaining regular follow-up, and going out of your way to provide them exceptional customer service. Your goal is not just to sell a vehicle. Your goal is to wow the customer while selling them the vehicle. That's one of the reasons behind our success. We've not only managed to survive in this business, we've also become the market leaders by treating people right.

Before we formally begin, let me get something out of the way. When I say you need to treat your customers properly, I hope it goes without saying that you cannot satisfy *all* of those customers. No matter what you do, there will always be that five percent of your customer base that you can never make happy. Some people are simply built that way. For others, the baggage of their expectations is too heavy to lift. Even the most successful companies I've seen cannot achieve a clean, 100 percent customer satisfaction rating.

Let's face it. There's a lot of negativity in the world. But that shouldn't stop us from being positive. Sure, some customers are difficult to deal with. But that doesn't mean we should stop working hard. In fact, if the customer presents a challenge, you must be willing to make the extra effort to present a solution. If they require extra attention and demand extra effort, that's exactly what you should provide. When the dust settles, they will come back to you, however begrudgingly. Ignore the negativity, and focus on the positives. Focusing on surviving in the midst of adversity can get you out of any sticky situation.

The rest of the chapter will focus on the importance, the basics, and the specifics of treating people right. Here we go.

THE SIGNIFICANCE OF TREATING PEOPLE RIGHT

We have all heard how important it is to treat your customers the right way. However, most have never stopped to consider a basic question: Why? Why is it so vital to the successful conduct of business? What exactly does it yield? Asking such fundamental questions may seem like a waste since all of us know, at a high level, that exceptional customer service is beneficial for business. But we should also consider some of the finer details of the big picture. By truly understanding why good customer service is important, we can come up with tailored strategies that help us achieve that level of service. When we know the results, we can determine how to go about achieving those results.

Here are some of the reasons you should treat your customers properly.

REPEAT BUSINESS

Let's begin with the most obvious of reasons, which is, incidentally, also the simplest one. If you treat the customers right, they will come back to buy. If you treat them right again, they will come back again. It's the circle of life for a car dealership. It's a major determinant of long-term success. Customers are the foundation of any sales organization, and by accumulating more and more of them, the foundation will get stronger and stronger still. Your repeat clients are your first and foremost resource. You can delve into this resource in a time of crisis. It's something to fall back on when all else fails. Even if the economy is in shambles and you don't acquire a single new customer in a month, you still have a steady support base—made up entirely of repeat clients—on which you can rely.

Your loyal customers are not only significant from a sales perspective. They can also help your organization improve its processes. They can take your whole team to the next levels. Sales is a mutually beneficial relationship—and not just in terms of product and profit. It's a constant give and take of value. You provide your clients value by selling them products and providing excellent service, and they provide value to your organization through constant feedback. They tell you what's right and wrong, what you should do, and what you should avoid. You won't follow through on all your customer's suggestions, obviously. But you'll at least have a pool of suggestions to draw from. You'll have enough to compare and contrast in order to pick the best option from a wide range of choices.

REFERRALS

You can't solely rely on repeat business. Eventually, the stream will run dry, and you'll run out of both clients and options. Remember that your goal is not simply to survive. It's to grow. And in order to do that, you need a healthy supply of new clients while retaining your relationship with the previous client base. This works particularly well in the current economic situation in which all of us find ourselves. Your older and newer client bases go hand-in-hand. When you're facing a reduction in new customers, who better to contact than your previous, loyal, clients for help?

We will discuss some of the best ways to secure referrals later in the chapter. For now, let's confine the discussion to how referrals benefit your business.

The first and most significant benefit of the referral mechanism is that it makes your sales cycle much more efficient and much less costly. It's a lead generation process for which you don't have to spend a considerable amount of time gathering prospects and calling disinterested individuals. The hottest leads come to you rather than the other way around. And when you do less, you spend less. Could there be a better alternative?

Another, often overlooked aspect of referral marketing is customer satisfaction. Behind every referral, there is a satisfied customer. If your approach is to secure more referrals, you need to strive for even greater customer satisfaction. It's a continual, self-perpetuating cycle. Referrals beget referrals. A few satisfied customers lead to even more. And, eventually, you will see a drastic improvement in your dealership's customer satisfaction rating.

There is statistical evidence that proves that referrals can bring in significantly more business. According to research, the closing ratio for leads generated through conventional means is a mere 10 percent, which is poor compared to the whopping 60 percent closing ratio with the referred leads. So, in short, referrals bring in more business, save time and money, help establish a huge network, and increase customer loyalty. Ignoring this step means taking the longer route which can, at any point in time, lead to a dead-end.

The Basics of Great Customer Service

Before moving on to some of the specific steps that will help you and your organization, it's important not to forget the basics. These are some of the principles upon which you can build the foundation of customer satisfaction. The basics are just as important as the specifics, if not more so. The basics lay down a path ahead of you. The specifics inform you how to tread the path. So let's consider these 10 steps to treating people right.

HAVE A STRONG WORK ETHIC

How do you define a work ethic? What are its key elements? In a way, all entries in this list are one or the other element of a professional work ethic. Making an effort, maintaining strong body language, and having passion and energy for what you do are all important aspects of the work ethic. So, in turn, the discussion of treating people right is a discussion about maintaining a strong work ethic. There are, however, some aspects of the subject that warrant further discussion.

Some of these aspects are what I like to call the three Ds of a strong work ethic: Dependability, Dedication, and Determination. Any professional salesperson is an invaluable asset to the team. Dependability is his vital attribute. The essence of dependability is an unspoken sense of responsibility and acting in accordance with that. But, dependability doesn't develop in a vacuum. It requires dedication. When you're absolutely dedicated to your job and your company, you'll inevitably be dependable. These two elements, therefore, go hand-in-hand. However, what makes the trio complete is determination. The determination to achieve your sales target, to rise above in the ranks of your organization, is what makes a successful salesperson.

But what has all this got to do with customer satisfaction? The three Ds of work ethic seem more like individual attributes of a good salesman. Yet what makes a good salesperson if not the ability to treat people properly? Without that, no one can be an asset to the sales team. Customer satisfaction is a by-product of a salesperson's dedication to the business. You will hardly ever find a single dedicated sales person who cannot treat people right. Rising in the ranks of your organization is nearly impossible without treating people right. In short, treating people right is all about work ethic.

BE ON TIME

Steve Jobs once said, "My favorite things in life don't cost any money. It's really clear that the most precious resource we all have is time." Considering his views, it's not hard to imagine why he was so spectacularly successful. We often hear phrases like "time is important" or "time is money." The simplicity and seeming obviousness of these phrases are the reasons we often take them for granted. But this very same simplicity holds the key to profound truths about success in business. The significance of being on time is one of those truths. A good salesperson—the one who generates the most customer satisfaction—is always on time.

One of the most unacceptable issues when running a business is a salesperson who is late. It is not allowed, under any circumstances whatsoever. When it comes to selling 1000 cars per month, time is literally money. Wasting that precious time is like throwing money away. More than that, it's a reflection on your personal and professional character. In today's economic climate, where gaining repeat business is already a Herculean task, you cannot afford to lose customers over such easily avoidable mistakes.

A common misconception among sales people is that being on time means arriving on the dealership floor on time. I won't disagree with anyone who suggests doing so is a significant positive. In fact, I'll be one of them. However, anyone who believes that this is the only way to be on time is hugely mistaken. In your sales career, you may face two kinds of situations. First, when arriving for appointments when being on time is a must. Second, when making a follow-up call, where being on time—though not necessary by any means—can create a significant advantage. You must consider both situations equally important.

MAKE AN EFFORT

There could not be any more obvious advice than this. It doesn't take a genius to figure out that making an effort is key to success. Everyone knows that. What most people don't know is how to make an effort and which areas require the most effort. Treating people right does not just require hard work; it requires smart work. That's what you do by finding the right avenues to invest your energy. Doing that requires great amount of thought, skill, and consideration. You need to make an effort to make an effort.

The first step is to identify your weaknesses. Which areas require the most attention? Which steps are the most critical when it comes to treating people right? These are crucial questions to consider at this stage. If you skip this step, you'll end up wasting a significant amount of time and resources on non-essentials, and that's the last thing you need. Identifying weaknesses depends on the amount of data you collect about your sales process. This data can be qualitative or quantitative.

Fact, figures, and statistics are examples of quantitative indicators. How many sales did you perform in a month? What's your customer satisfaction ratio? As important as graphs and numbers is qualitative data; the qualitative data provides you with the reasons behind the numbers. If the sales numbers are low, why is that? If the customers are disgruntled, what's the reason? You can gather qualitative data through internal or external sources. For instance, the management's set of observations of sales conduct is an internal source. Customer feedback, on the other hand, is an external source.

When you have enough data to proceed, you can identify the areas where you need to make the most effort. You also need to find the best ways to ensure progress. Quantitative data can help narrow down the range of areas on which to focus. Qualitative data can inform your next steps. For instance, if your customer satisfaction ratings are low compared to your competitors, you have an area on which to focus. However, the actual feedback of customers

204 | CHRIS MARTINEZ

on how you can improve your sales process is a valuable guide.

USE EFFECTIVE BODY LANGUAGE

Body language is a salesperson's weapon. In fact, it is one of the most effective weapons in your arsenal. Still, many salespeople ignore its importance. Rather, they invest most of their energy in learning more about the product or working on their demonstration, woefully unaware of the fact that their body language is what turns customers off in the first place. Proper body language is how you put customers at ease. It's how you influence people to make a decision. When done right, proper body language is a way to penetrate their subconscious. But how exactly do you do that?

Good body posture is all about maintaining a balance. You must be welcoming in your posture. Lean forward and open your arms. It is a symbol of your strong commitment and keen interest in the conversation. Avoid being too overbearing or having an overwhelming presence during the interaction. Give customers space to think, consider, and discuss. You need to exude confidence with every step, but avoid appearing overconfident or pushy. Smiling is important to put the customers at ease, but you also need to convey to the customers that you take their concerns seriously.

There are many do's and don'ts of body language and perfect posture. Remember not to point or use dramatic hand gestures to accompany speech. Pointing fingers can be considered rude, whereas hand gestures can be too distracting. Don't speak loudly enough that it's annoying or quietly enough to be inaudible. Don't speak so quickly that you're unintelligible or so slowly that the process is tedious.

Keep a soft tone of voice, one that is calm and reassuring. Maintaining positive eye contact with customers is a must. It builds engagement with the customer and makes you seem less hostile and negative even if you are disagreeing with the customer.

Other than focusing on your own posture, you also need to pay attention to the customer's body language. Observe how they stand, how they speak, and how they interact with each other. The customer's body language informs you about the nature of the conversation. It also helps you to determine the next task. For instance, if the customers are too defensive, you need to penetrate their defenses. If they are too aggressive, you need to calm them down. When you use proper body language and correctly interpret the physical signals the customers send toward you, half your job is already done.

BE FULL OF ENERGY

Your body language is a channel through which you can express your energy. That energy is critical for the customer experience of buying your products. When you sell a car, you're not just selling. You are putting on a performance. "All the world's a stage, and all the men and women merely players," said Shakespeare. When you sell, you are a player, and the dealership floor is your stage. The amount of energy you bring to the stage will determine how much your performance will be appreciated.

It is understandable that, being the emotionally fickle creatures that we are, it's impossible to be energetic at all times. No one's asking you to do that. But any successful salesperson, like any successful performer, has the unique ability to be able to turn the energy level on and off. Any successful salesman you observe is proactive, and energy is infectious. You're not only responsible for looking enthusiastic and eager to serve the customer. You also lift the spirits of your customers, in a way. It's a beautiful process. You can make a customer's miserable day better with your energy level, so it's a way to make the customers happy while generating profit at the same time.

MAINTAIN THE RIGHT ATTITUDE

There are two ways to look at maintaining the right attitude. Both are equally important and deserve the same attention. Attitude, like energy, is something you take to the customer. And maintaining the right attitude can create vibrancy in your interactions with the customer. This is the first sense of the word. Your attitude is reflected in the way you treat your customers. It is a big part of the interactions that precede a sale. And, given its importance, you need to devote extra attention to doing it right. Maintaining the right attitude with the customer is the first half of the equation.

The second way to look at attitude is with regard to the attitude you bring to work. The right attitude makes professional sensibility. Are you committed to reaching your goal? How do you interact with your fellow coworkers? The internal dimensions of being a salesperson are as important as the external dimensions. After all, you cannot succeed in any profession without having the right attitude. If the key to maintaining the right attitude with the customers is belief in the product, belief in the company can make you a better employee. Believing in the company means having faith in its values. It represents making an effort to reach goals the company has set. Having the right attitude can enable you to form healthy relationships with both your coworkers and the management, and these relationships are the backbone of any successful organization.

BE PROFESSIONAL

What springs to your mind when you consider someone who is "professional?" Is it the way someone talks? Is that the way he dresses and carries himself? In most situations, these considerations, although important, are superficial. They can enhance your professional image, but they don't form the backbone of it. The key to having a professional approach to business lies elsewhere. By some definitions, being professional is all about maintaining a strong work ethic. That's what most people refer to when they say someone is a pro, and being a pro is another important component of treating people right.

What are the characteristics of professional salespersons? What distinguishes them from non-professionals? Once you know the answers to these questions, you know what to aim for. Above all else, professional salespersons take responsibility. They take responsibility for their own actions and any other mistakes committed by their team. They don't make excuses or back down from a situation. Instead, they welcome challenges and see them as opportunities. Perhaps the biggest difference between professional and non-professional salespersons lies in how they treat their customers. Professionals ask questions. They follow through. They keep their promises. That's how they keep customers.

BE PASSIONATE

If being professional means doing what your job requires you to do, being passionate means rising above your duty and giving more. While the dictionary defines passion as a powerful emotion or feeling, passion is much more than that, and it affects many areas of professional activity. Being passionate improves your sales numbers, commitment to the job, dedication to the company goals and, most importantly, interaction with the customers. This is why being passionate is such an integral step of treating people right. Without it, it will be difficult for you to succeed as a salesperson.

When I entered the car sales business, I wasn't remotely interested in it. I never considered it as my long-term career option. Slowly, as I spent a few years in the business, the spark of sales inside me began to grow. The time when I began to act upon my curiosity to learn more about the business was the same time when I realized the importance of being passionate. As I observed my co-workers, a distinct pattern began to emerge. My fellow salespeople who treated their job like a job did fairly well. But, those who were truly passionate and committed to the sales process outperformed the rest by miles.

One of the results their passion brought to the table was increased customer satisfaction. How, I wondered, did that happen? I searched and searched for answers, keenly observed their methods for days, weeks, even months, but to no avail. I discovered no hidden trick or technique that improved their numbers. It was not until I had some experiences of my own as a customer that it all came together. It was not any secret trick or hidden talent that made them such effective salespersons. It was a pure, unadulterated passion for sales.

As a customer, interacting with salespersons who followed a professional approach versus those who followed their hearts were widely different experiences. With the former, I felt like we were performing a business transaction, which we were. But with the latter, there was a clear sense of joy. Buying was not a mere business transaction. It was something much more than that. It was an experience. It was then that I realized the value of passion. And I have followed that since.

BE COACHABLE

If you ask someone what's the most important requirement for learning new professional skills, most would say it's a skilled teacher. Few respondents venture to suggest that you, yourself, need to be willing to learn. More than willingness, you must have the ability to learn. Yes, learning is a skill in and of itself. You need to learn that skill if you want to succeed. You need to be coachable if you want to learn to treat your customers properly. How do you learn to be coachable? What qualities do you need to possess to be able to achieve that?

The first step to being coachable is allowing others to challenge your beliefs and pre-conceived notions about sales. Be open to questioning your beliefs yourself. That is the key to learning more. It brings a much-needed flexibility to your attitude. If you're not capable of having your beliefs challenged, you cannot grow as a profession-al. You can never truly learn how to treat people right. What you think is the right way to deal with customers may be the very issue that is holding you back. You need to step out of your shoes and learn to view the problems from the perspective of others.

Once you are able to accurately identify the problems, you need to learn to take action. It's important to learn to do things differently and continue to consistently improve upon your habitual practices. Be willing to stop habitual practices that don't work and adopt new ones. Otherwise, challenging your beliefs and letting others challenge you will all be for nothing. All your efforts, passion, and commitment will go to waste. You won't be able to grow professionally. You surely wouldn't want that; you want to grow. You want to treat people right. So you need to go out and do it.

Being coachable doesn't just mean listening to professional mentors. That may be an important aspect of learning, but it's not the only one. It involves constantly searching for good advice, which may come from anywhere. Can you think of a dependable resource other than management or professional mentors? If you answered, "Yes, the customers," you're on the right track. When it comes to treating people right, who better to learn from than the customers themselves? They are the key to unlocking the secrets of customer satisfaction. Customer input is a valuable learning resource.

How do you receive that input? You can classify customer feedback into several categories: primary or secondary, formal or informal, and direct or voluntary. Every means is an equally valuable pathway to gain insight into the customer mindset. You can formally request customer feedback on your services, which is the most effective way to create a learning experience. Your customers are the best judges of what you did right or did wrong. When it comes to treating people right, they determine the best practices. Your job is simply to follow those practices.

There's also another, much more underappreciated, way to receive input from the customer, and that is involuntary feedback. Some of the most skilled sales professionals make it their hidden weapon. Even if the customer does not explicitly provide formal feedback, there's still a lot to learn from their body language and general demeanor. It's through the observance of their attitude that the best sales professionals shine. They can immediately identify problems and rectify them. They know if the sales process is working or not, and they can resolve any issues that may arise before things go too far. This process is known as dynamic learning. You learn while you're selling.

DO A LITTLE EXTRA

Taking action is important, but the extent of the action you take is even more important. Are you willing to go out on a limb? Are you comfortable travelling that extra mile to get ahead of the others? You may think being a better salesperson is all about the quality of service, and that isn't incorrect. But, it's about the quantity of service as well. How much you do is as important as how well you do it. That's why, in order to truly treat people right, you must do a little extra.

What is it that you need to in terms of "extra?" In short, everything. You need to invest more into all aspects of your job. From the number of work hours to increasing sales numbers, you should put in that extra ounce of effort. In terms of customer satisfaction, we must consider how to do extra when it comes to customer service.

Customers have an in-built sensibility that recognizes when a salesperson is doing merely what they're required to do versus rising above their duty and delivering more. You need to lead to succeed. Identify what some of your competitors are doing. Exceed their efforts to deliver that truly "wow" experience to the customers and, trust me, they'll realize it.

Doing a little extra, when it comes to customer service, involves going out of your way to accommodate the wishes of your clients. It includes making an effort to gain new customers and preserve current ones. For instance, you need to make an effort to add value to your follow-up emails.

Why should the customers waste their time reading emails sent just to "touch base?" Why not include a comprehensive and informative resource to help clients choose their next vehicle? These considerations are significant in order to ensure maximum customer satisfaction.

You must aim to understand the customers' needs and desires. Know their expectations, and attempt to exceed them. If the customer asks you for a favor, grant him two. If the customer requests a moment of your time, be generous. If he has any complaints, thoroughly address and mitigate them. This is how you win people over; it is the way to treat people right.

KEEP GROWING

When we embarked on our journey, we had no clue what we were getting into, no mentor to guide our steps, and no one to correct our mistakes. The only things we possessed were a desire to grow our business, a passion to achieve our goals, and a desperate need to do anything and everything to succeed. It was this commitment to our cause that was a major reason for our success. And success we had. In our first month alone, we were able to double the existing numbers. Customers came in droves and went home satisfied. It was a thing of beauty, the definition of perfection.

We didn't stop at perfection, however. We had a drive not just to achieve once but to keep achieving, more every month. Doubling the sales figures in a month was a spectacular achievement, and we were undoubtedly proud of it. But we didn't let pride get in our way. Even if we had stopped there, the company would have been more profitable than it had ever been before. But, that was not our approach.

We had to keep growing; that was our goal. Our goal was to never stop, and we're still pursuing that goal to this very day.

If you want your organization to grow and succeed, you need to keep track of the numbers. These numbers will guide your way, push you to try harder, and inform you of successes. Let's look at the numbers we started with at Charles Maund. When we joined the store, it was selling almost 150 cars each month. However, within the first two months, we were able to increase their output to the point where we were selling 300 cars a month. This was closer to the nationwide car sales target. Most dealerships across the country aim to sell around 350 cars per month, and are happy when they reach that target. But the nationwide average is way below that. As surprising as it may seem, a lot of dealerships in the country sell around 150 new and 50 used cars in a month.

Compared to my suggestion of aiming to sell 1000 cars per month, these numbers may seem ridiculously low. You may think that, after reading this book, car sales will spring to action and the market situation on the ground will transform instantaneously, skyrocketing above the competition. But no such thing will occur, I assure you. I have no expectations of glory or delusions of grandeur because I maintain a healthy level of skepticism, despite my firm optimism. I know that the average salesperson does not have the desire or the incentive to challenge himself. And it's not due to a dearth of helpful sales advice. Many experienced salespersons have written much more authoritatively and eloquently on the subject. So, a lack of encouragement is not the problem for an average salesperson. The issue is that he simply doesn't want to push himself to higher limits.

My bosses referred to this phenomenon as "financial complacency"—a term I've grown to like. It perfectly encapsulates the mindset of salespeople who simply refuse to grow. They find solace in mediocrity and are perfectly content to secure a particular place in the community and cling to it. This kind of self-satisfaction is poison for a business. If you don't constantly attempt to grow, everything you have built for yourself over the years can instantly go up in flames. Financial complacency is why many organizations suddenly, and quite shockingly, find themselves out of business. They may not be able to explain the cause, but I can. It is because of being financially complacent.

When you reach a particular position in your business, you cannot afford to stagnate or be complacent. You have to be constantly engaged in an upward struggle. You have to reach the next level. The next level is not simply an abstract term for success. It's a set of definable goals that you must achieve. Growing your business is a constant process of setting goals and setting out to achieve those goals. For instance, if you want to reach the next level, you need to expand your dealership space, increase the staff, and acquire increased inventory.

All this reminds me of the often misunderstood line from Kevin Costner's film, *Field of Dreams*: "If you build it, they will come." Most dealerships follow this as their mantra. They spend an average of five years in planning mode. They estimate and determine where their next location will be. They go on to build the location with the right strategy and sell around 150 cars a month. There are even more dealerships that sell only 20-60 cars a month. What they lack is the courage to grow. And, yes, it takes plenty of courage to grow. You need to be confident in your abilities and not refuse to grow.

Let me provide you with an inspirational example. Longo Toyota in California is one of the best dealerships in the world. They are currently selling around 1800 new cars and 500 used cars in a month. This didn't happen overnight. They worked hard to secure their position in the car sales community and have worked even harder to sustain that position for decades. They've remained in the top spot since 1967 because they've never been afraid to grow. They've grown so much that they have dominated the market for the past 50 years. They simply refuse to leave the number one position.

Dealerships like Longo Toyota inspire me. Whenever I'm in need of inspiration, I look toward their strategies and feel reinvigorated. Doing that provides me with a new spirit, an incentive to repeat their success—and even exceed it—in Texas. Regardless of a national financial recession, you can find a way to grow. If people hesitate to buy cars, you can find a way to still sell them. The important point is, you must try. Try hard, and never quit—despite the difficulties, despite the criticisms.

Naysayers and cynics will try to stop you and will put obstacles in your path, but it's your job to ignore the negativity and embrace the positivity. Your job is to go out and do the impossible.

Knowing why to keep growing is important, no doubt about it. But knowing how to keep growing is what we're all after. It's what sales is all about. You need to redefine your sales process to be able to achieve success and not stop once you do. What's sorely needed is a new strategy, a new approach—not to mention, renewed vigor. You need to be able to look the challenges in the eyes, and make the impossible possible. Here are some of the key steps that may enable you to do that.

BEGIN WITH A VISION

If you asked me about the single most essential prerequisite for business growth, I'd respond with just one word: vision. With a sound, consistent vision, you can build your organization from the ground up and take it to the moon (and back). Without a vision, you're in deep, deep trouble. A vision not only paves the way forward, it brings consistency to your organizational processes. Without one, you'll be stranded in a fast-paced market, utterly directionless. Without vision, your organizational process will be neither here nor there. That's the importance of beginning with a vision.

Consider any great entrepreneur who built his respective organization and led it to be the most successful of all time in its industry. Every one of them had specific talents, and they all succeeded. The nature of their businesses likely varied, but there was one thing they had in common. People like Bill Gates, Warren Buffet, Mark Zuckerberg, and Steve Jobs all began with nothing but a vision. They didn't have the financial or physical resources when they started. Their only resource was their brain. They had a wealth of ideas, and they built multi-billion dollar companies on the solid foundation of their sound vision. That is the secret of their success. Of course, suggesting that is the only reason is too simplistic. There were undoubtedly other factors involved, but the vision was what held it all together.

The kind of vision you set out with is also an important consideration. After all, this is the determinant of success or failure, so it merits considerable attention. There is no perfect dictionary definition for "vision" in this context, but there are certain common characteristics that you might find in many visionary ideas. Some of these characteristics include a passion for what you do. This passion can be instinctual, or it can be acquired. If you are passionate enough to achieve a goal, you'll find ways to do it.

There is then the matter of the goal itself. What is it that you're setting out to achieve? The answer is a big part of the vision. The goal, however, is never static. Neither Bill Gates nor Mark Zuckerberg knew what he would eventually become. They knew what they each liked, and they wanted to achieve success doing what they loved. By doing that—and doing it well—they rose to their present positions. Your goal can be as vague as setting out to dominate the market or as specific as selling 1000 cars per month. It doesn't matter. What matters is that you have enough will power and resources to achieve it.

INVOLVE THE RIGHT PEOPLE

What's a vision without those willing to achieve it? What's passion without those who are passionate? The correct answer, of course, is "nothing." A vision may belong to one single person, but no single person has been able to successfully run an organization single-handedly. It requires a concerted effort. Therefore, a team is as important—if not more so—than the one who leads it. This is why you need to involve the right people in your operation. The right team can take you to your goal and beyond. Once you begin to perform and the gears settle into place, you can be an unstoppable machine.

If you want to grow, you need to surround yourself with people who have the same vision as you. One of my great friends gave me advice that I will never forget and that I've tried to implement in my everyday work process. He said, "Eagles don't fly with Buzzards." Like attracts like. People with shared values have proven to work together in harmony. Finding the right people is one of the most important requirements for business growth. The key to success is not only to remember that fact but also successfully implement it in your business practices.

ALWAYS BE PREPARED TO TURN IT UP A NOTCH

Growth, by definition, is a state of constant upheaval. It is the antithesis of a status quo, the opposite of a static state. Sometimes, you'll hear the gentle hum of constant anxiety. Other times, you'll feel the violent jolt of a sudden flurry of activity. In the state of constant motion, you can never afford to stay in one place for too long. You must always be prepared to take the next step. You're on the journey of your life, and you constantly need to put one foot in front of the other. It's a steep climb uphill and the surface is such that, if you pause, you fall. You need to constantly be on the lookout for the slightest chance of improvement. As soon as you find the right moment, seize it.

Imagine the process of growth as a series of steps. Once you build a good foundation at each interval, you're able to push to the next level. If this means finding a second location to hold more inventory for customers, that's what you must do. Despite the spectacular success we've achieved, I constantly continue to push the boundaries of what we can do. I continue to aim for more and then do more once we've achieved that. I'm currently looking for another lot because we now have new goals. We want to reach 1500 cars per month, and we will continue to push and increase our actions to hit higher levels than our store and Austin, Texas has ever seen.

BE ORGANIZED

Are you, as a person, constantly on the edge Do you struggle to stay organized even in the most basic situation? If so, you may not be fit to run an organization, or you may require major assistance. Organization is one of the central aspects of success. It's what allows you to stay on top of things. It's what enables you to drive the organization, not the other way around.

It's sad to see many business managers fail to perform well in such a basic area. Let me put it simply: If you don't stay organized, you cannot grow. It's as simple as that. How can you expect to meet complex challenges and solve intricate problems if you're not organized? How can you keep employees in line and maintain discipline when you so woefully lack it? It's impossible to struggle to manage your affairs and the organization's affairs at the same time. Plain and simple, you must be organized.

How do you stay organized? Is there a strategy, a defined set of steps that enables you to do that? Strictly speaking, there isn't. But, there are many common actions that will ensure a method to the madness and an element of stability amidst all the chaos. For instance, making to-do lists is a simple way to maintain a set of tasks in one place, and check off those you have performed. It not only makes you more organized, it enables you to keep track of daily activities. It makes sure that you don't miss anything and that you perform all tasks that are crucial for the smooth functioning of your business.

Organization is all about getting into a flow. It's about repeatedly performing a series of motions so that a routine sets in and performing those activities seems as easy as slipping on a pair of well-worn shoes. When it's that easy, you know you're on the right track.

PROVIDE GREAT SERVICE

What truly makes an organization grow? Some would say competitive prices; others would point to great products; many would recommend a perfect process; a few would suggest the team's professional skills. All of them would be glossing over the most critical reason behind an organization's growth and progress. That reason is: the customers. Customers are the driving force behind any organization. They're the foundations on which any business stands and runs. Without them, there are no products and no lucrative prices. If they don't choose to buy, why should we ever learn to sell? Without them, there is no business. Without them, there is no us.

In our frantic struggle to engage in business competition and perfect the logistical support necessary to sustain the competition, we often forget why we're here. We're here for those who choose to step out of their homes, visit our dealership, and pay our salaries. We owe not only our success, but also our existence as a business, to these customers. Working hard on your products, process, and people while ignoring customers is like going for a walk to stay healthy but forgetting to breathe. Yes, it's that important. Customers must be any organization's number one priority. Yet, in reality, they rarely are.

We must aim to provide the best service possible to customers. Their satisfaction runs the business, and their disapproval can destroy it. Therefore, every aspect of our sales process should be designed and improved with the customer in mind. For instance, if we're aiming to improve efficiency, we need to define efficiency through the customer's perspective, not our own. Convenience in business is for the customers, not for the salespeople. Even the incentives for the salespeople should be defined by whether or not they attract more new customers or satisfy the existing ones. If every aspect of the business is designed for the customers, there's nothing that can stop your business from growing.

I have devoted a considerable portion of this book to discovering and describing ways to ensure customer satisfaction. No matter how much I write, it won't fully emphasize how significant it is to keep the customers happy. It is your ultimate goal, and without it, you can't reasonably even imagine selling 1000 cars per month.

PREPARE TO MAKE SACRIFICES

When it comes to finding ways to succeed, Napoleon Hill summed it up when he said, "Great achievement is usually born of great sacrifice." Take this proclamation, and make it your working principle. If you operate everyday with a "no pain, no gain" philosophy, you'll see a marked change in the performance output. The irony is that when you put yourself on the line and risk everything, only then do you stand to truly gain from it. You win when you're prepared to lose. That's why you have to prepare to make sacrifices.

It's simple when you really consider it. Selling 1000 cars per month appears an impossible task under normal circumstances. In today's economy, where businesses put in all their energy into simply surviving and getting from one day to the next, you're seeking to tread an entirely separate path. Not only do you have to simply survive, you also have to grow your business operations to ten times their current size. Some may call it madness, yet it takes a certain touch of madness to achieve the unachievable. The inner desire, the desperation that propels you to succeed, might also drives you away from other things. You can't have everything in life, at least not all at the same time. And there will come a point, in your pursuit of the big goal, when you will need to make some choices.

The sacrifice can be of any nature. The pressure of work may strain your health. It may drive you apart from your family. It may leave you with less time to pursue other life goals. But isn't that the definition of an obsession? Can an obsession ever be healthy? To be clear, I'm not asking you to shun your life in the line of work. This is not war, and you're not a potential martyr. All I'm asking you to do is be prepared. Be prepared for what may come your way. Be prepared to sacrifice. It's not a must; it's a may. But, however distant that possibility may seem, you must be prepared to embrace it.

The sacrifices you prepare for do not necessarily have to be of a personal nature. You may be required to let go of certain members of your team, even those you personally like. That is a sacrifice. As a manager, you are responsible for making certain difficult decisions, and you're not a good manager if you don't make them. That's sacrifice. Are you willing to make it?

STAY FOCUSED

Another by-product of intense dedication is intense focus. These two elements go hand-in-hand. One is nothing without the other. You have to stay focused on the goal if you want to succeed. Otherwise, your job involves more than ceaselessly going around and around in circles, not knowing where to go or what to do next. You cannot afford that, not when your aims are so high and everything is on the line. You need to stay focused, not only for yourself but also for those who depend on you—your family, your employees, your co-workers and, most of all, your customers.

For some, staying focused and not losing track of goals is easy. Focus comes naturally to them. It's an instinct, born from their infatuation with success. For others, however, acquiring that razor-sharp focus is hard. They have to work hard to maintain it, develop a habit by pushing themselves every moment of every day.

It might surprise you to learn that I was in the latter category. When I entered the industry, I had no prior interest in car sales. I had no drive and no desire to perform at my absolute best. But I kept at it, one foot in front of the other. I walked—albeit slowly at first. I failed. But I didn't give up. And I'm now in a position to advise others who wish for the same success I'm experiencing.

Focus is also associated with success. As I started to achieve more, I wanted to go even further. When I had success, I had an incentive to push myself beyond my limits. The lesson is, don't give up if you don't sell 1000 cars in your first month. Learn to celebrate the small victories, and don't stop there. As you sink deeper into the depths of your endeavors, you'll find yourself rising up, elated, and closer to your eventual goal. That's the key to developing focus and achieving success. You have to be more and more involved in what you do, take interest, build a passion for it, go out there, and achieve it.

BE CREATIVE

When you're on a difficult journey on the path to success, who says you cannot have a bit of fun along the way? It not only makes your ride more enjoyable, it also takes you further than you might imagine. Be creative in your approach to sales. Identify innovative solutions to exasperating problems. Create a collaborative process, and involve your employees in the decision-making process. Why should the customers be left behind? Bring them into the fold as well. When you begin to enjoy what you do, you'll see an outburst of creativity envelop your organizational processes.

Other than allowing you to have fun and enjoy the ride, creativity serves a practical purpose. It might be cliché to say we're living in the era of creativity. But the fact of the matter is, it's absolutely true. Look all around you. Take in the colors around you. Pay attention to the messages. Modern-day advertising is being propelled by a swarm of creative individuals. It's a living, breathing organism, and no two breaths are the same. Amidst all the creative outpour, you're trying to sell vehicles. Most of dealerships in your surrounding area likely sell the same products. Why will people buy from some and leave others alone? Consider that question. You have to find that unique quality that customers can see in you. You have to be creative to get your voice heard above all the commotion. Otherwise, you'll find yourself drowning in a sea of color and noise, and you won't be able to do anything about it.

WORK SMART

Theodore Roosevelt once said, "Far and away the best prize that life has to offer is the chance to work hard at work worth doing." It's a phenomenal piece of wisdom, while I won't disagree, his is not the only advice you need to consider. Working hard is a crucial prerequisite to success, but it's not the only thing that will propel you toward your target. Some would suggest working smart is just as important as working hard (if not more so).

In simple terms, working smart means setting SMART goals for yourself—Specific, Measurable, Attainable, Relevant and Timely goals. Many, in their blind passion to achieve success, set unimaginably high goals for themselves, and then beat themselves down every day, working hard, giving everything to achieve those goals. Despite all their efforts, they find themselves nowhere near their goals. Weeks, months, years, even decades later, they finally break. Giving up their pursuit, they believe that they were simply not cut out for it. This is the worst kind of failure—the debilitating, humiliating, haunting kind that leaves you unwilling to move forward and unable to go back.

Before you set out on a journey toward your destination, ask yourself whether you're headed to the right place. More importantly, determine whether or not you believe you can reach it and what will take to get there. It may be tempting to think that you'll be the next Bill Gates or Warren Buffet if you work hard enough. But, most people ignore the fact that Bill Gates didn't set out to be Bill Gates. Warren Buffet didn't begin his business to be one of the richest people in the world. They are individuals with a unique set of talents, a passion for what they do and, most importantly, a smart approach to achieving their goals.

Therefore, if you want to grow your business, you need to reconsider your goals. Are they too lofty? Are they ultimately unachievable? If so, you need to bring them in line with the SMART strategy. Let's break the term apart and analyze what SMART goals are:

SPECIFIC

This is the first step to redefining your goal. A healthy goal needs to be specific. Being the best car dealership in the world is an admirable ambition. But it's not specific enough. What makes a car dealership the best in the world? Is it the sales numbers or the customer satisfaction ratio? What is it that you want to achieve? In our case, it's increasing the sales numbers. Beyond that, we're aiming to reach a particular number: 1000 cars per month. This is an example of a specific goal.

MEASURABLE

The whole point in setting a specific goal is that we can constantly measure our progress against it. By setting measurable goals, we know exactly where we stand at any given moment and what we need to do to move closer to the goal. It brings out our flaws and errors and shows us the way forward. If you have a measurable goal, you must also possess the requisite tools to constantly gauge your performance.

Sharpen your analytical skills, and make use of all the relevant statistics if you want to measure your sales performance. Constantly set standards, and make an effort to rise up to those standards. You're working hard here, too, but at least you know exactly what you're working hard to achieve.

ATTAINABLE

"Anything is possible." Isn't that the mantra on which the American dream is built? If you develop a vision and a focus, if you work hard with skill and dedication, anything is possible. Any goal is attainable. Why, then, do I include attainability as a critical attribute? What we need to focus on is not attainability alone. It's the relativity of attainability. Rather than asking yourself whether or not your goal is attainable, you need to consider how attainable it is. By setting specific, measurable, and achievable goals, you can pave a pathway to success.

RELEVANT

When you have a whole lot of tasks to complete, it's easy to get disoriented in a flurry of activity and, ultimately, lose your way. You need to be absolutely sure whether or not your goal is relevant to your ultimate destination. Why are you doing what you're doing? Why do you want to achieve what you want to achieve? These are crucial considerations. You need to stay on track and seek to achieve goals that enable you to do that.

TIMELY

How long might it take to reach your goals and achieve what you want to achieve? Timeliness of the goals is an important consideration. Set timeframes for yourself and your team. How many months will it take to double the number of cars you sell? How many months will it take to triple it? Time is a unit of measurement, and you must assign it the utmost importance.

KEEP DETAILED RECORDS

Keeping detailed records of all aspects of business activity enables you to achieve two of the aforementioned requirements to continue growing: staying organized and setting measurable goals. Without this resource, all you can do is grope in the dark, desperately clinging to the hope that you'll find a way. Hope is no good here; you need assurances. Will you find the way? How will you find it? The answer depends on the extent of your record keeping.

You will need to record everything. From inventory information and customer contact details to market trend statistics and notes on customer follow-up, you must keep detailed records of everything. If resources allow, you can create a separate department for information management. Otherwise, assign this crucial task to the IT or another department. However, without a functioning information management mechanism, you cannot expect a smooth road going forward.

Your records will help you analyze sales performance and see where you stand. Even a monthly set of statistics can enable you to accurately gauge the dealership's performance as a whole. For example, if your car sales numbers are exactly where you want them to be but your customer satisfaction ratio lags behind, you know there is room for further improvement and you know where it must be focused. To be even more specific, you can rely on detailed customer feedback in order to pinpoint precisely where the fault in your service lies. Is it the way you demonstrate, or is it due to the lack of the follow-up? A combination of qualitative and quantitative information is extremely effective when it comes to an accurate appraisal of the unique problems that may arise in the organizational processes and the specific solutions you need to come up with in order to do away with those problems.

Imagine a scenario without any of these statistics. Do you know where you stand? Do you know what needs to be righted? No matter how brilliant a manager or salesperson you may be, you rely on these records to keep you going. A plumber, no matter how skilled, cannot mend pipes with his bare hands. Why, then, is it reasonable to expect good results when we're not willing to make the effort to achieve them? Remember the difference between hard work and smart work. Sales managers who put all of their energy into working hard to improve the efficiency of the processes are good managers, no doubt. But, those who divide their time and focus into both the assessment of the process and the practical implications of that assessment are those who truly rise above their duty and take their organization to the next level.

ANALYZE YOUR COMPETITION

A crucial component of the records you keep is information on your competitors. Everyone keeps records of their business activity, at least on some level. But how many of us analyze the performance of our competitors in addition to that of our own organization? It is amazing how some of the steps to which many of us pay such little attention can play such a huge role in the growth of an organization. Sometimes, it's the things we ignore or take for granted which make a world of difference. Analyzing the competition is one of those things. It's absolutely essential, yet often nowhere to be found when it comes to actual practice.

When you analyze your competition, the sources on which you rely are essential. Where do you get your information? Which pieces of information are the most valuable? These are crucial considerations. For instance, some of the obvious sources are the direct ones. Reading their annual reports to assess their sales numbers and quarterly revenues is a good idea. Keeping tabs on their marketing activities and promotional offers is another effective way to compare and contrast their processes with yours. In addition, there is the ever-reliable resource: customer feedback. You can simply ask customers who've had experiences with both dealerships what they think of those respective experiences.

Analyzing your competition enables you to set a performance threshold. If you're behind it, you need to reach that threshold. If you're ahead, you need to exceed it. Remember, your goal is not to compete with other dealerships; it's to dominate the market. You cannot do that without keeping tabs on the activities of your competitors.

Conclusion

My 13+ years of experience in the car sales industry have been a whirlwind of challenges and a rollercoaster ride of ups and downs, twists and turns, and a general sense of joyous excitement. It's been an emotional journey. I've both gained and lost plenty. Above all, it has been a truly incredible learning experience. Over the course of these 13+ years, I've grown from a timid, over-enthusiastic rookie salesman to a confident and authoritative manager.

The transformation didn't occur overnight. It took years of acquired knowledge and professional experience, some of which I acquired through my mistakes and some through learning from others' experiences. Isaac Newton claimed, "If I have seen further it is by standing on the shoulders of giants." In the course of my professional career, I have stood on many such shoulders, shoulders of better, greater salespeople than I am.

Collective knowledge—isn't that what separates humans from other species? We build on our existing knowledge. We take our collective wisdom and add to it—that's how we make progress. That's how we are no longer rubbing logs to build fire. Through this book, I've attempted to add my meager contribution to the all-consuming, all-encompassing pool of sales knowledge. The content of this book won't, on its own, revolutionize the act of selling a product. I have no such expectations. But I do cling to the hope that this book will inspire at least one timid, young salesperson to come into his or her element and, hopefully, after an illustrious career, continue to inspire others to do the same. If you believe, after reaching the book's conclusion, that my own journey of inspiration has come to an end, I can assure you that it has not. It has, in fact, only just begun.

57980294R00144